Scepticism, Rules and Language

Scepticism,
Rules and Language

G.P. Baker & P.M.S. Hacker

Fellows of St John's College, Oxford

Basil Blackwell

First published 1984
Basil Blackwell Publisher Limited
108 Cowley Road, Oxford OX4 1JF, England
Reprinted 1985

British Library Cataloguing in Publication Data

Baker, G. P.
  Scepticism, rules and language.
  1. Wittgenstein , Ludwig. Philosophical
  investigations
  I. Title   II. Hacker, P.M.S.
  149′ .94   B3376.W563P53

ISBN 0–631–14703–9

Typeset by Oxford Verbatim Limited
Printed in Great Britain by
Billing and Sons Ltd, Worcester

Contents

Contents

Preface

While we were engaged upon the preliminary research for the second volume of our *Analytical Commentary on Wittgenstein's Philosophical Investigations*, Professor Saul Kripke published his much discussed lecture, 'Wittgenstein on Rules and Private Language'. In this long essay, he gave a controversial sceptical interpretation to Wittgenstein's remarks on rules and rule-following in the *Philosophical Investigations* §§143–242. By coincidence we happened at this time to be combing through Wittgenstein's *Nachlass* in search of the sources of these remarks. And it was evident that Kripke's interpretation flew flagrantly against Wittgenstein's manifest intentions in these important passages, misconstruing their meaning, mis-identifying their target, and misrepresenting their thrust. Kripke's lively discussion had a counterpart in Professor Crispin Wright's *Wittgenstein on the Foundations of Mathematics*, which explored similar sceptical views in connection with Wittgenstein's philosophy of mathematics. 'Wittgenstein's rule-scepticism', his 'rule-following considerations', were obviously attracting much attention in the philosophical community, and we were tempted to turn aside from our main concerns in order to try to prevent these misunderstandings from becoming a new orthodoxy in the interpretation of Wittgenstein. Consequently, when Professor Wright invited us to contribute to a *Synthese* volume of essays on Wittgenstein, we succumbed to temptation. The result was the first essay in this book: 'On misunderstanding Wittgenstein: Kripke's private language argument', which is to be published in 1984 and is reprinted here by kind permission of the editor.

We had initially thought to let matters rest there. For we had shown that Wittgenstein's arguments were antithetical both to the rule-scepticism that he was supposed to have invented and also to the sceptical solution which he allegedly proposed to meet this new form of scepticism. However, reactions to our paper, which we read to the Oxford Philosophical Society in May 1983 and presented to our graduate seminars in Oxford, stimulated us to reconsider our initial decision. For while it was generally conceded that, as an interpretation of Wittgenstein's analysis of rule-following and private language, Kripke's arguments were wrong, nevertheless (we were told) rule-scepticism, the rule-sceptical considerations, and above all the community-view resolution(s) of them were exceedingly profound. This novel form of scepticism, even if Wittgenstein did not invent it, seemed very deep to many, and its implications far-reaching.

It is *prima facie* surprising that this new form of scepticism should attract so much attention, let alone appear profound. The suggestion, stated baldly, that I cannot be sure that I now mean by 'plus' or 'red' what I meant by it yesterday seems neither plausible nor very interesting. The proposition that I can never be sure, *really* sure, what another person means by his words looks like a stale rehash of scepticism about other minds. In the light of the ease with which we can find out (determine what it is to comply with) the rules of, say, chess or the traffic code, the proposal that what counts as following a given rule is in principle opaque appears bizarre rather than persuasive. But it is clear that these rule-sceptical considerations hit a sympathetic chord in the sensibility of contemporary philosophers.

The explanation for this is in fact at hand. Rule-scepticism was expounded against a philosophical and cultural milieu in which it was becoming commonplace among avant-garde intellectuals to conceive of a language as a highly complex calculus of rules, and to conceive of understanding as a hidden process of operating this calculus or depth-grammar. The rules of grammar which constitute the 'theory of meaning of the language' are, of course, not explicitly known to anyone. Unlike the humdrum rules of language we teach children, they are objects postulated by the transformational-generative grammarian, the cognitive psychologist or the philosophical semanticist. Consequently they are treated as explanatory hypotheses forming part of a scientific explanation of the workings of language and of the hidden mechanisms of understanding. Rules which no one cites in explanations of the correct thing to do, which no one refers to in justifying what he has done or in criticizing others who have acted incorrectly, which need high-powered philosophers and linguists to discover them, and which, once formulated, are unintelligible to most people who allegedly follow them, are indeed dubious objects. Small wonder that rule-scepticism seems a deep and relevant philosophical concern!

When rules are transmogrified into explanatory hypotheses, scepticism about rules emerges as a rephrasing of the now-orthodox scepticism about natural laws – a rerun in modern dress of Goodman's 'New Riddle of Induction'. Any experimental evidence, as all good scientists and philosophers of science assure us, underdetermines any explanatory hypothesis. No mathematical function is uniquely determined over an infinite domain by any finite listing of pairings of values with arguments. Because functional dependences are held to be the canonical form for stating scientific laws, this mathematical theorem has the substantive consequence that any explanatory generalization is underdetermined by any body of observational data. Indefinitely many distinct hypotheses will fit all of the facts available. This sceptical reasoning is immediately applicable to any 'theory of meaning for a language'. The data for the construction of such a theory are overt linguistic performances (linguists would include 'linguistic intuitions' so-called); from these finite data the grammar, the system of rules, conceived as an explanatory hypothesis, has to be constructed. And it is immediately obvious that, so conceived, it is underdetermined by the data. Only one step further, and the shared understanding presupposed by ordinary linguistic intercourse is rocked to its foundations. For it seems that speakers can be said to understand each other if and only if they operate the *same* calculus of rules (theory of meaning). Identifying understanding with tacit (unconscious) mastery of a semantic theory makes mutual understanding highly problematic, and mutual understanding cannot be vindicated by pointing out that people *seem* to understand each other. (The dilemma is similar to Locke's: to ground understanding in simple ideas in the mind opens the door to doubt whether different persons attach the same ideas to any word.)

Against this cultural context it is not surprising that rule-scepticism should appear a deep issue. The postulates of cognitive psychology, theoretical linguistics and (on some versions) philosophical semantics seem to be called into doubt. So even though proponents of 'Wittgenstein's rule-scepticism' would not dream of presenting their arguments as attacks on modern linguistic theories, nor consider them as a *reductio ad absurdum* of such theories, they manifestly cast a shadow over the proceedings which are taking place centre-stage. This makes sense of the appeal (or threat!) of a form of philosophical reasoning that would otherwise seem unmotivated and devoid of interest (save as a mistaken interpretation of Wittgenstein).

Rule-scepticism, then, threatens to force upon us the conclusion that shared understanding is altogether conjectural (or, pushed to even more absurd consequences, that language, meaning, understanding, are impossible). The advertised 'sceptical solution' (wrongly attributed to Wittgenstein) purports to escape from this unpalatable conclusion by proposing a reconstruction of the notion of objectivity in respect of the claim that it is an objective matter whether or not two people communicate in speaking the same language: agreement with the behaviour of the majority of one's linguistic community is the yardstick of correct understanding, or at least a surrogate for the putative fact of mutual understanding which is taken to vindicate judgments that one understands an expression correctly. This too, in the present context, is bound to have substantial appeal.

Both rule-scepticism and 'the community view' (the sceptical solution) claim that something is wrong with the concepts of understanding and communication. But if rule-scepticism unadorned by a sceptical solution is not problematic but absurd (as we argue), there is a more straightforward response, namely to call into question the analyses of the concepts of understanding, a rule, and a language which are essential to the derivation of the absurdity. What rule-scepticism effects is not the sawing off of the branch on which Everyman is perched in virtue of employing our ordinary concepts of understanding and communication, but rather the sawing off of the branch on which philosophers and theoretical linguists are sitting in virtue of analysing the concept of understanding a language in terms of implicit knowledge of a complex system of semantic rules. Theories of meaning are dead branches in the Tree of Knowledge. Rule-scepticism, if cogent, would threaten to prune away this rotten material, and a sceptical solution is a futile attempt to restore it to life by propping up one dead branch with another.

The incoherence of the enterprises of philosophical theorists of meaning and of theoretical linguists (in particular transformational-generative grammarians of various types) was a large subject to which we had already dedicated a book (*Language, Sense and Nonsense*). We had no desire to repeat ourselves. But the suggestion that the rule-sceptical considerations were, irrespective of whether Wittgenstein had propounded them or not, a singularly profound contribution to philosophy was a different matter. This seemed a new misunderstanding which needed eradicating.

Accordingly we wrote the second essay in this book 'The illusions of rule-scepticism'. Our primary concern here is to uncover the roots of rule-scepticism and to display the rot that infects them. It is indeed correct that rule-scepticism has not been properly appreciated by a critic who simply finds it an absurd fad in modern philosophy. On the other hand, its significance has not been fathomed by those who purport to find it so important; for they steadfastly refuse to consider the lesson that it might teach, namely that rule-scepticism is the surface manifestation of deep-rooted misunderstandings characteristic of the present day. It requires uprooting, not by-passing. The sceptical solution is an absurd answer to an incoherent question. And finally, it is not only that the roots of rule-scepticism are infected, but also the soil which nurtures them is poisoned. Out of the assumptions that a language is a system of rules which speakers tacitly know, that understanding consists in the unconscious operation of this hidden calculus, and that explanations of meaning consist of model-theoretic correlations of words with entities in reality, nothing healthy can ever grow.

The final essay, 'Rule-scepticism and the harmony between language and reality', rounds off the previous two by taking up three items of unfinished business. The first is to sketch an answer to the nagging question 'What then is the strategic purpose of the rule-following considerations in the *Philosophical Investigations*?' The second is to make it intelligible that philosophers, in addressing rule-scepticism, should have mistaken a conceptual muddle for a genuine problem. And the third is to throw some light on what it means to claim that rules are internally related to their applications. Though seemingly independent, these topics are closely related. Wittgenstein's remarks about rule-following are identified as one facet of his general concern with what he called 'the harmony between language and reality'. Allied discussions focus on the pictoriality of the proposition and the intentionality of desires, intentions, expectations, etc. In each of these cases philosophers are tempted to interpose abstract or mental entities to explain an internal relation (e.g. between a proposition and the fact that makes it true or between an expectation and the event which fulfils it), not recognizing that every such relation is perspicuously forged in language. The supposition that an interpretation, whether a personal or community-wide one, must mediate between a rule and its application is a parallel illusion of Reason.

The strategic purpose of the 'rule-following considerations' is to clarify the conceptual connections of meaning with the use and with the explanations of expressions. It is natural to view explaining a word and using it correctly as two independent, unrelated criteria of understanding it (or grasping its meaning). This error is a special case of the misconception that understanding a rule and knowing how to apply it are two quite separate issues. Rule-scepticism runs off the rails at the very outset by treating the question of what acts are in accord with an understood rule as an open one. In sober truth, to understand a rule *is* to know what acts would count as compliance with it, just as to understand a statement is to know what would be the case if it were true. In overlooking this internal relation between rules and their applications, rule-scepticism is shown to be as firmly rooted in conceptual confusion as are familiar, venerable forms of scepticism.

Bede Rundle and Stuart Shanker kindly read these three essays. We are grateful to them for much thoughtful criticism and helpful advice.

G. P. B. & P. M. S. H.
St John's College, Oxford
1983

*Le plus grand défaut de la pénétration n'est
pas de n'aller point jusqu'au but, c'est de
le passer.*

La Rochefoucauld

1

On Misunderstanding Wittgenstein: Kripke's private language argument

1 'Wittgenstein's argument as it struck Kripke'

After a long period of neglect, Wittgenstein's discussions of rule-following have, in the last few years, received some serious attention. This has been stimulated partly by a growing interest in his philosophy of mathematics, partly by the publication of the enlarged edition of his *Remarks on the Foundations of Mathematics* which includes a fifty-page section on rule-following. Perhaps the most important stimulus, however, is the conviction among many philosophers that the confrontation between realism and anti-realism, between truth-conditional semantics and semantic theories involving the notion of assertion-conditions, is *the* fundamental issue in contemporary philosophy. Accordingly the early Wittgenstein is strapped to the truth-conditions bandwagon, and the later Wittgenstein, strait-jacketed within the confines of anti-realism, is harnessed to the assertion-conditions one. Since his remarks on rules have a clear bearing on issues which interest participants in this confrontation, they have become the focus of extensive discussion.

Saul Kripke's essay 'Wittgenstein on Rules and Private Language'[1] applies this currently popular picture of

[1] This essay criticizes Kripke's article in *Perspectives on the Philosophy of Wittgenstein*, ed. I. Block (Blackwell, Oxford, 1981), but for the reader's convenience we have given page references to the later version published as a

Wittgenstein's early and later work to a reconsideration of the famous private language argument in the *Philosophical Investigations* §§243ff. The discussion of rule-following which *precedes* the private language argument (§§143–242) is the focal point of his examination, and from it he draws a variety of original and controversial conclusions. Rather disarmingly, he suggests at the outset that 'the present paper should be thought of as expounding neither "Wittgenstein's" argument nor "Kripke's": rather Wittgenstein's argument as it struck Kripke'.[2]

To use the writings of a philosopher as a Rorschach spot is perfectly legitimate. But there is an ever present danger that one's ruminations will be taken as descriptions of the spot. Indeed, in the course of his reflections Kripke attributes to Wittgenstein a variety of views which he never held, and imposes upon his writings a variety of interpretations for which there is no licence. In this paper we shall try to differentiate sharply between Wittgenstein's argument as it struck Kripke and Wittgenstein's argument, and to demonstrate that on the salient issues Wittgenstein's argument not only differs from, but actually confutes Kripke's picture.

More than mere exegetical correctness is involved here. Kripke is surely right in thinking that §§134–243 of the *Investigations* contain some of the most original and significant philosophical reflections written this century. If the line of argument pursued in them is valid, their implications, both within philosophy and without, are considerable. Modern philosophical logic, theoretical linguistics, as well as branches of empirical psychology would stand in need of re-evaluation. So it is important to understand what Wittgenstein was arguing. Only then we can assess it, and see where we, and others, stand.

---

book, with minor alterations, several new footnotes, and an added postscript: Saul A. Kripke, *Wittgenstein on Rules and Private Language: an Elementary Exposition* (Blackwell, Oxford, 1982).

[2] Kripke, *Wittgenstein*, p. 5.

Kripke's interpretation of the core of the *Philosophical Investigations* is as follows. The 'real private language argument' is not in §§243ff., but in §§143–242. Indeed the *conclusion* of the private language argument is stated in §202:

> And hence also 'obeying a rule' is a practice. And to *think* one is obeying a rule is not to obey a rule. Hence it is not possible to obey a rule 'privately': otherwise thinking one was obeying a rule would be the same thing as obeying it.

The problem which Wittgenstein confronts in these hundred sections is, Kripke claims, a sceptical one. The discussion of the rule for forming the series of even integers is designed to raise the question of how I can know whether my current use of a word (e.g. 'plus') coheres with what I previously meant by it, given that my current use is (or can always be made out to be) a novel application. Nothing in any instructions given to me (or which I give myself) forces me to go on '1002, 1004', rather than '1004, 1008'. The instructions I gave, the examples I produced, can be made out to be consistent with both ways of proceeding. Equally, nothing in my mind constituted the fact of my meaning myself to go on thus or otherwise. (I didn't run through an infinite series in an instant and the formula I had in mind has no magical powers to generate the answer.) Scepticism about being able to know whether I am using a word in accord with what I meant by it leads to the paradox stated at §201:

> This was our paradox: no course of action could be determined by a rule, because every course of action can be made out to accord with the rule. The answer was: if everything can be made out to accord with the rule, then it can also be made out to conflict with it. And so there would be neither accord nor conflict here.

So epistemological scepticism about applying a word in accord with what one means by it leads to the conclusion that there can be no meaning at all, and language is impossible. This paradox is 'perhaps the central problem of *Philosophical Investigations*'.[3]

Wittgenstein, according to Kripke, gives a 'sceptical solution', of a Humean form, to his sceptical problem. This strategy consists in accepting the sceptic's premises but denying that the sceptical conclusion follows from them. So Wittgenstein agrees that there is no fact-in-the-world that constitutes meaning something by one's words. But this annihilates the possibility of meaning only on the assumption that sense is given by truth-conditions (i.e. correspondence to possible facts-in-the-world). He allegedly repudiates this theory, replacing it by the picture of sense as determined by conditions for assertion. The assertion-conditions for my meaning W by 'W' are my being inclined to apply 'W' thus-and-so, given that the rest of the community is too. In these circumstances there is no reason to *deny* that my current ('novel') application of 'W' accords with what I (and others) previously meant by 'W'. Therefore meaning something by a word requires a community to supply agreement and to prevent thinking one is following a rule and following a rule from collapsing into each other. Hence 'it is not possible to obey a rule "privately" ', and the conclusion of the private language argument is really stated before what goes by the name of 'the private language argument' has even begun. This does not, however, preclude our conceiving of Robinson Crusoe meaning something by his words as he talks to himself on his desert island. For in so conceiving of him 'we are taking him into our community and applying our criteria for rule following to him'.[4] A physically isolated person can follow rules, but a person considered in isolation cannot.

This sketch provides the bare outline of Kripke's colourful painting. We shall fill in more detail only where necessary.

[3] Ibid., p. 7.
[4] Ibid., p. 110.

2 Scepticism about Wittgenstein's 'sceptical problem' and 'sceptical solution'

Although Wittgenstein found some of the problems of scepticism interesting, even revealing (as in *On Certainty*), anyone familiar with Wittgenstein's work will feel sceptical about the suggestion that he made a sceptical problem the *centre-piece* of his *chef d'oeuvre*. In his very first philosophical notes he wrote against Russell:

Scepticism is *not* irrefutable, but *obvious nonsense* if it tries to doubt where no question can be asked.

For doubt can only exist where a question exists; a question can only exist where an answer exists, and this can only exist where something *can* be *said*.[5]

In his last notes on certainty he wrote:

The queer thing is that even though I find it quite correct for someone to say "Rubbish!" and so brush aside the attempt to confuse him with doubts at bedrock, – nevertheless, I hold it to be incorrect if he seeks to defend himself (using, e.g., the words "I know").[6]

It would be very surprising to discover that someone who throughout his life found philosophical scepticism *nonsensical*, a subtle violation of the bounds of sense, should actually make a sceptical problem the pivotal point of his work. It would be even more surprising to find him accepting the sceptic's premises, the 'doubts at bedrock', rather than showing that they are 'rubbish'.

Initial qualms may be strengthened by reflection on the oddity of the so-called scepticism. What is classically known as

[5] Wittgenstein, *Notebooks 1914–16* (Blackwell, Oxford, 1961), p. 44.
[6] Wittgenstein, *On Certainty* (Blackwell, Oxford, 1969), p. 65.

scepticism typically involves challenging an apparent evidential nexus. The sceptic agrees that we *do* know the truth of statements about subjective experience, but, since they do not entail statements about objects, he denies that we really know anything about the material world. In a more obliging frame of mind, he accepts the possibility of knowledge about the behaviour of others (or about memories and current evidence, or singular statements) but denies that it supports cognitive claims about other minds (the past, inductive generalizations). But Kripke's sceptic, unlike the classical sceptic, saws off the branch on which he is sitting. For he is not claiming that certain *given* knowledge fails to support other commonly accepted cognitive claims. His conclusion is not that he certainly means either a or b by 'W', but cannot be sure which; nor is it that he knows what he now means, but cannot be certain whether it is the same as what he meant yesterday. Rather he concludes with 'the paradox' that there is no such thing as meaning, so language cannot be possible. But *this* is not scepticism at all, it is conceptual nihilism, and, unlike classical scepticism, it is *manifestly* self-refuting. *Why* his argument is wrong may be worth investigating (as with any paradox), but *that* it is wrong is indubitable. It is not a sceptical problem but an absurdity.

To defend common sense presumably means to find good reasons why what we ordinarily and more or less unreflectively believe is true, and is known to be true. Kripke's Wittgenstein[7] is a common-sense philosopher, holding that philosophy only states what everyone admits. He resembles Hume, who wrote, 'Should it here be asked of me . . . whether I be really one of those sceptics, who hold that all is uncertain . . .; I should reply, that this question is entirely superfluous, and that neither I, nor any other person was ever sincerely and constantly of that opinion.'[8] The similarity with Hume allegedly reaches deeper, since Kripke's Wittgenstein pursues

[7] Kripke, *Wittgenstein*, p. 63.
[8] Hume, *A Treatise of Human Nature* I iv 1.

a Humean strategy of giving a 'sceptical solution' to his sceptical problem, i.e. he concedes that the sceptic's negative assertions are unanswerable, but contends that our ordinary belief is nevertheless justifiable, because it does not require the justification the sceptic has shown to be untenable. The switch from truth-conditional semantics to assertability conditions is argued to effect just this move.

The analysis is wrong on several counts. First, Hume does *not*, in his analysis of the self, objectivity, and causation, defend common sense. He is not claiming that philosophy never casts doubt on the rational justification of ordinary beliefs, but that philosophy is impotent to *change* them. The famous passage Kripke quotes continues thus:

> Nature, by an absolute and uncontrollable necessity has determin'd us to judge as well as to breathe and feel . . . Whoever has taken the pains to refute the cavils of this *total* scepticism, has really disputed without an antagonist, and endeavour'd by arguments to establish a faculty, which nature has antecedently implanted in the mind, and rendered unavoidable . . .
>
> . . . If belief, therefore, were a simple act of thought without any peculiar manner of conception, or the addition of a force and vivacity, it must infallibly destroy itself and in every case terminate in a total suspense of judgment. But as experience will sufficiently convince anyone who thinks it worthwhile to try, that though he can find no error in the foregoing arguments, yet he continues to believe and think and reason as usual, he may safely conclude, that his reasoning and belief is some sensation or peculiar manner of conception which 'tis impossible for mere ideas and reflections to destroy.

Hume insists that we have *no* good reason to believe in the existence of objective particulars, no good reason to believe that our several perceptions belong to a unitary self; etc. Far from defending 'common sense', he insists that *all* the arguments are on the side of the sceptic. Rational investigation *proves* that the fundamental beliefs of 'common sense' are *fictions*, generated by the workings of the imagination according to natural laws of mental association.

Second, Hume's 'sceptical solution' does *not* consist in giving a *justification* for our ordinary beliefs, i.e. rational grounds showing them to be well-founded. Rather, he defends a radical split between theory and practice, between Reason and Nature. Though every argument speaks against belief in objectivity, this *cannot affect our beliefs*. 'Philosophy would render us entirely Pyrrhonian were not nature too strong for it.'[9] He denied the Pyrrhonist thesis that sceptical arguments will lead to suspension of belief and *ataraxia*. Belief is not determined by Reason, but by Nature. Hume was indeed not trying to *subvert* our beliefs, but to show that they are determined, non-rationally, causally, by Nature *against* Reason.[10]

Third, not only is Hume thus misrepresented, but so also is Wittgenstein. He insisted that he was *not* defending any *opinions*: 'On all questions we discuss I have no opinion; and if I had, and it disagreed with one of your opinions, I would at once give it up for the sake of argument, because it would be of no importance for our discussion.'[11] Nor was he defending common sense, if that means: giving reasons for believing that material objects exist independently of our perceptions of them, or that other people enjoy experiences, or that we mean things by our words, etc. Rather the task, in this respect, consists in showing that the philosophical puzzle (of scepticism, idealism or solipsism) rests on systematically traversing

[9] Hume, 'Abstract of Treatise of Human Nature'. Cf. *Enquiry Concerning Human Understanding* v 1, xii 2.

[10] 'Nature has not left this [belief] to his [the sceptic's] choice, and has doubtless esteem'd it an affair of too great importance to be trusted to our uncertain reasonings and speculations' *Treatise* I iv 2.

[11] See Wittgenstein, *Wittgenstein's Lectures, Cambridge 1932–35*, ed. A. Ambrose, (Blackwell, Oxford, 1979), p. 97, also *Wittgenstein's Lectures on the Foundations of Mathematics, Cambridge, 1939*, ed. C. Diamond (Harvester Press, Sussex, 1976), p. 103.

the limits of sense. His purpose was the investigation of ordinary *concepts* which are used in the expression of common-sense beliefs. But he was not concerned to defend those beliefs, rather to clarify those concepts. For the problems of philosophy arise through the distortion and misuse of ordinary concepts, and the way back to sanity consists in obtaining an *Übersicht* of the problematic expressions.

Finally, Kripke contends that in the course of his 'sceptical solution' to his 'sceptical problem' Wittgenstein in effect denies some of our ordinary beliefs, contrary to his principle that 'If one tried to advance *theses* in philosophy it would never be possible to debate them, because everyone would agree to them.'[12] Wittgenstein is forced to do this because he *accepts* the apparent sceptical denials of our ordinary assertions, and he only saves himself from blatant inconsistency by 'cagily' refusing to state his conclusions in the form of definite theses or straightforward formulations. It is, in fact, this caginess that explains his inability to write a work with conventionally organized arguments. What 'thesis' is Wittgenstein supposed to be propounding here? According to Kripke, 'Wittgenstein holds, with the sceptic, that there is no fact as to whether I mean plus or quus'.[13]

This is quite wrong. If Wittgenstein had claimed that when A told B to expand the series '+2', A did *not* mean B to go on '1002, 1004 . . .', he would be denying what we all admit. But he does not claim this: 'Certainly; and you can also say you *meant* it then; only you should not let yourself be misled by the grammar of the words "know" and "mean".'[14] And if A meant such-and-such, then, Wittgenstein might add, it is a fact that he meant such-and-such (see below). What Wittgenstein is denying is a *philosophical* claim, viz. that the 'act of meaning'

[12] Wittgenstein, *Philosophical Investigations* (Blackwell, Oxford, 1953), §128.

[13] Kripke, *Wittgenstein*, pp. 70f.; 'quus' is a function defined by: $x \otimes y = x + y$ if $x, y < 57$, otherwise $x \otimes y = 5$. This is Kripke's operative example for the paradox involved in rule-following.

[14] Wittgenstein, *Philosophical Investigations*, §187.

effects miracles, such as traversing an infinite series in a flash, and a *philosophical* thesis, viz. that my meaning such-and-such is a fact-in-the-world (or more specifically, a fact-in-my-mind), and that my justification for saying that I meant addition by 'plus' is that I have observed this fact in my mind. To deny this is not to deny what we all admit, but to deny a nonsensical metaphysical theory.

The considerations so far are merely intended to foster *prima facie* doubts about Kripke's interpretation. It is, we suggest, implausible (though not impossible) that Wittgenstein should find sceptical problems and Humean sceptical solutions the fountainhead of philosophical insight. But there is a far greater likelihood that he would concur with Dr Johnson's ironic remark about sceptics: 'Truth, sir, is a cow, which will yield such people no more milk, and so they are gone to milk the bull.'

3   The 'paradox'

The interpretation of *Investigations* §§201–2 is crucial for Kripke's case. For the 'paradox' of §201 is 'perhaps the central problem' of the whole book, and the conclusion of §202 ('it is not possible to obey a rule "privately" ') is not an anticipation of the private language argument,[15] but a statement of its conclusion, based on arguments already given. By §243 the impossibility of a private language has already been proved. The core problem is, according to Kripke, a *normative* version of Goodman's 'new riddle of induction'. No past fact about my mind or my behaviour constituted my meaning W by 'W', so nothing in my present use of 'W' can constitute accord (or conflict) with what I meant by 'W' (the meaning I assigned to 'W'). So I cannot know that in my current use I am still using 'W' with the same meaning. But not even God, were He to peer into my mind, could know this. So there is no such thing

---

[15] Kripke, *Wittgenstein*, p. 3.

as using a word in accord with a rule (with the meaning one gave it), no such thing as meaning something by a word, and hence no such thing as a meaningful language. This is the 'paradox'.

There are reasons for doubting whether §§201–2 are the pivotal remarks of the book. Also reasons for doubting that they are the culmination of a sceptical argument, or that they incorporate a refutation of the possibility of a private language. And there are alternative interpretations of the remarks which rest on better exegetical evidence. Finally, there are doubts whether Kripke's 'problem' is coherently stateable. These considerations strengthen the doubts sown in the last section.

The history of §§201–2 The *Philosophical Investigations* Part 1 went through four typescript stages, dated 1938 (TS 220 in von Wright's catalogue), 1942–3 (TS 239), January 1945 (the 'Intermediate Version'), and 1945–6 (the printed version TS 227).[16] The Intermediate Version is *almost* identical with the final version in respect of argument from §1 to §217, but it *does not contain §§201–3*. So although the Intermediate Version contains the whole of the *argument* prior to §§201–3, it does not incorporate the 'conclusion' of the argument which, according to Kripke, is the pivotal point of the book. Moreover, the Intermediate Version contains the bulk of the private language argument,[17] and if §§201–3 already establish the conclusion *of the private language argument*, and §§243ff. only examine a potential counter-example to the argument concerning sensations, it is odd, to say the least, that Wittgenstein omitted the *punctum saliens* in this draft.

Further light is shed on the matter by the *immediate* manuscript scource, MS 129 (pp. 119ff.), which was written from

[16] For the detailed account of this complex bibliographical history, see G. H. von Wright, 'The Origin and Composition of the Philosophical Investigations' in his *Wittgenstein* (Blackwell, Oxford, 1982), pp. 111ff.

[17] The missing remarks, inserted only in the final draft, are: §§247–52, 257, 262–9, 292, 294, 297, 299–301.

17 August 1944 onwards. Equally illuminating is the more remote manuscript source, the pocket notebook MS 180(a), which contains material transcribed into MS 129.

In MS 129 the context of the occurrence of §§201–3 is a discussion of how I know that this is red, i.e. what is now *Philosophical Investigations* §§377–81 (which also does not occur in the Intermediate Version). The argument is concerned to establish that judgments such as 'These images are identical' or 'This is red' do not rest upon *recognition*. It runs as follows: How do I know that this is red? One is inclined to say – I look at it and see *that it is red*. But how does this wordless seeing–that–it–is–red help me if I do not know what to say, how to express this 'recognition' in words? And sooner or later I must make the transition to using an expression. And at *this* point rules leave me in the lurch (by themselves as it were, they hang in the air). All teaching, at the end of the day, will not help me in this respect, for it cannot relieve me of the task of applying the rule, of 'making a leap' and *saying* 'This is red', or *acting* in a certain manner (which comes to the same thing). It is of no avail to try to interpose, between looking at an object and saying that it is red, a (bogus) recognitional stage of 'seeing that it is *this*',[18] for now one would need a rule to effect the transition from this 'seeing that it is *this*' to saying it is red.[19] But *this* transition would be a 'private' one and the only rule which could guide it would be a private ostensive definition determining what *this* is. Yet justification must be public (cf. *Philosophical Investigations*, §378).

At this point in MS 129 we have what is now §201 ('This was our paradox . . .') which began with Wittgenstein's remarking that he had found himself in the difficulty that it seemed . . ., which clause he then crossed out and replaced by 'This was our paradox'.[20] This clearly refers back to what is

[18]   Cf. MS 180(a), 68f.

[19]   Or indeed to effect the transition from seeing that it is *this* to seeing that it is red! And what *is* the *this* which this is?

[20]   In MS 180(a), 72, the passage began by Wittgenstein's remarking that he was (earlier) in the difficulty that a rule could not determine any action,

now §198, which occurs earlier in the manuscript (p. 25). Why this allusion to these earlier difficulties at this point? Because the issue is similar, and the conclusion of §198 can be brought to bear on the present problem. §198 argued that the connection between the expression of a rule and the act which counts as accord with the rule is forged, *inter alia*, by training. We are taught that acting *thus* in response to such-and-such is correct, and anything else incorrect. We explain and justify *this*, but not another thing, by reference to the rule; and so on. To follow a rule is a custom; it involves a regular use of the expression of rules in training, teaching, explaining, and in giving reasons. Now Wittgenstein embroiders on these observations in the new context of a discussion of recognition and the unmediated application of 'red' and 'same' (as well as 'same image' and 'red image'). The 'earlier difficulty' that a rule could not determine what to do in accord with it, the 'paradox', was evidently a misunderstanding. This is shown by the fact that no interpretation, i.e. no rule for the application of a rule, can satisfy us, can definitively fix, *by itself*, what counts as accord. For each interpretation generates the same problem, viz. how is it to be applied?²¹ Now Wittgenstein adds a new point to the argument of §198, deepening the implications of the claim that what counts as following a rule is fixed by a normative regularity. What the absurd paradox that rules cannot guide one *shows* is that how one understands a rule need not be an

---

since anything can be brought into accord with the rule. There PI §198 occurs on page 1.

²¹ That in the argument preceding §198 in the final text there was, on more than one occasion, an insoluble regress of interpretations, is evident, e.g. how the teacher *meant* the pupil to continue cannot be what determines what counts as accord, since what he meant can be differently interpreted (§§186f.); the general formula of a series cannot determine accord, since it too can be variously interpreted (§§189f.; cf. §146). It is not wholly clear whether in MS 129 the successive proposals 'I see it as *this*' 'I see that it is *this* colour', 'I see that-it-is-red' etc. are conceived to be analogues of a succession of interpretations. Evidence in MS 180(a) suggests that this *is* Wittgenstein's drift of thought.

interpretation, but is manifest *in acting*, in what we call 'following the rule'. (The draft of §201 here is much the same as
the final version.) [22] That we have 'understood a rule in a
certain way', Wittgenstein continues ('Dass wir eine Regel
"aufgefasst" haben'), is shown *inter alia* in the certainty, the
absence of fumbling, in its application. Then follows *Investigations* §§202–3, i.e. *that* is why 'following the rule' is a practice.
How does this observation bear on the discussion of colour
recognition? It is simple: there can be no rule guiding the
transition from a seeing-that-this-is-so to saying 'This is red'
because there could be no technique of application for such a
rule, no normative regularity in its employment, no custom of
applying the word always in the same way, no practice (see
below). The 'private' following of a rule, e.g. a mental ostensive definition, that is presupposed by the supposition that
recognition intervenes between seeing and saying, is a sham,
in which following a rule and thinking one is following a rule
collapse into each other. The sequel continues to probe what is
wrong with the idea that recognition is the ground for judging
an object to be red, and develops into a discussion of seeing
aspects.

MS 180(a) is the source underlying MS 129 on this theme.
The longer discussion there begins with an examination of
aspect-seeing (pp. 52ff.): do I *interpret* the figure now thus,
now otherwise? Do I see everything always *as* something? Do
I need words for such 'visual interpretation' or are words only
necessary to communicate what I see? This evolves into a
discussion of my judgments about my visual images, and
thence into a long investigation into how I know that *this* is
red. The key theme here too is to repudiate the suggestion that

[22] It is, however, noteworthy that in MS 180(a), 72 an alternative drafting
to 'And so there would be neither accord nor conflict here' was that 'accord'
and 'conflict' here lose their sense altogether, which does not imply a
paradox leading to the conclusion that language is impossible, but implies a
misunderstanding of what counts as acting in accord with a rule and what as
acting contrary to one. And what goes for MS 180(a) goes for the final
version too!

any recognitional process mediates between looking, and saying that this is red. Here occur early drafts of *Investigations* §§378–81 (in a different order). The draft of §201 (on p. 72) occurs after an examination of the following sequence of propositions: I see that it is red, but don't know what it is called! I see that it is this colour, and I know that *this* colour is called such-and-such. Which colour? I recognize that it is *this*. But now I must make the transition to words or deeds! After a draft of §201 Wittgenstein elaborates: the rules here leave us in the lurch because there is no (genuine) transition from seeing that this is *this* to seeing that it is *red*, there is no technique of application of a rule here. The 'rules' are free-floating. For this (pseudo-) transition is a private one. If the transition from looking at an object to applying the word 'red' cannot be made without mediation (by a recognitional process, or a private ostensive definition) then it cannot be made by means of a rule either. Consequently, 'to follow a rule' designates a practice, which cannot be replaced by the bogus appearance of a practice (cf. §202). This seems to abolish logic, he wrote in an early version of §242, but it does not. It is one thing to lay down methods of measurement, another to obtain results of measurement. But what we call 'measuring' is partly determined by a certain constancy in results of measurement.

What tentative conclusions can we draw from these data? First, the history of §§201–3 suggests that these remarks are *not* the pivot of the whole book. They were not incorporated in the Intermediate Version, which contained in completed form both the argument preceding §§201–3 and the bulk of the private language argument. Secondly, in their original context they quite explicitly build upon §198 *and* upon the senselessness of private ostensive definition, *as established by the private language argument*. Thirdly, their original purpose was to deepen the insight of §198 and to bring it to bear on fallacies concerning *recognition* as mediating between saying and seeing. It was not to defend a new paradox, viz. that there can be no such thing as following a rule. Fourthly, the manuscript contexts have nothing to do with scepticism in any shape or form, neither with sceptical problems nor with sceptical solutions. (Nowhere is it suggested that I do not know that poppies are red!) There is no evidence to suggest that Wittgenstein was concerned with a normative version of Goodman's 'new riddle of induction'. Fifthly, in its original contexts in both manuscripts the remark that following a rule is a practice has nothing directly to do with *social* practices. Its exclusive concern is with the fact that rule-following is an *activity*, a normative regularity of conduct which exhibits one's *Auffassung* of a rule, manifests how one understands a rule.

Do these sections incorporate the conclusion of the private language argument? This depends upon what one takes this conclusion to be! If it is held to be the contention that it is not possible to obey a rule 'privately', then, of course, it does. But that is unsurprising. More interestingly, in context, these sections do incorporate at least some of the conclusions of the private language argument, since *they explicitly presuppose them as having already been established*. And rightly so!

For the moment we claim not that this information is decisive, only that it is suggestive. It is possible, but improbable, that the repositioning of these remarks betokens a total reorientation of their sense. Perhaps, after composing the Intermediate Version, Wittgenstein suddenly realized that these two manuscript remarks, embedded in a discussion of knowing that this is red, concerned with dissolving confusions about recognition, in fact contained in crystallized form the core of his book.

The interpretation of §§201–2   A closer look at these crucial remarks in their final, different, context may strengthen our doubts. §201 paragraph (a) is clearly concerned with the question raised in §198(a), viz. ' "But how can a rule show me what I have to do at *this* point. Whatever I do can, on some interpretation, be brought into accord with the rule" ' (our translation). The problem here posed belongs to a series of closely interwoven questions running through §§139–242. If the first part of the book can be said to be concerned with uprooting the *Bedeutungskörper* conception of meaning in all its forms, this part is concerned with the more subtle *Regelskörper* conception. It aims to break the hold of a misguided conception of rules as mysteriously, magically, determining or constituting the meanings of expressions, and of understanding as a grasping of rules which then guide us along predetermined rails. The problem-setting context is as follows. Earlier, Wittgenstein has argued that the meaning of an expression is its use. Equally the meaning of an expression is what is given by an explanation of meaning (§75); and an explanation of meaning is a rule for the use of the expression. But how can such an explanation, e.g. an ostensive definition or a series of examples or a general formula, determine the complex use of an expression? For any rule can be variously interpreted. The statement of a rule is not a repository from which the use unfolds or a logical machine that generates applications of its own accord.

With respect to understanding, which is the correlate of explanation, the problem presents itself thus. We typically understand an expression in an instant. We can say what we understand by giving an explanation. But how can what is understood, grasped in an instant, be something like the use, the pattern of application of an expression, that is spread out in time (cf. §138)? And if what is understood is expressed by an explanation, a rule, how does that explanation, which can be variously projected, guide one in how one uses an expression? The apparent tension between these claims is the concern of §§143–242. This discussion falls into two main parts. The first (§§143–84)[23] explores the concept of understanding (with a long digression on reading)[24] and establishes that under-

---

[23] For detailed analysis of *Investigations* §§143–84 see G. P. Baker and P. M. S. Hacker, *Wittgenstein: Understanding and Meaning* (Blackwell, Oxford, 1980), pp. 621ff.

[24] Given that Wittgenstein's discussion of reading intentionally runs parallel to his analysis of meaning and understanding, it should seem puzzling to Kripke that Wittgenstein did not introduce a 'new paradox of reading', viz. that since reading is not just mouthing words while looking at

standing is not a mental event, state or process. Rather, to say of a person that he understands a word is to characterize him as having, at a particular time, a capacity, a mastery of a technique. Understanding is akin to an ability. The second part (§§185–242) clarifies the notions of an act's conforming (or conflicting) with a rule, and of an agent's following a rule. By particularization, this elucidates what it is for the use of a word to be correct (to conform to its explanation), and what it is to mean something and to understand an expression.

After exploring two pictures of how accord with a rule is determined, each of which was unsatisfactory, Wittgenstein faces the question of multiple interpretations head-on in §198. If whatever one does can be brought into accord with the rule on some interpretation,[25] how on earth can a rule guide one? (Note that this is the identical problem of §201(a).) The answer is given immediately, with no suggestion of an irresoluble paradox that needs to be sidestepped. We ought not to say that because whatever we do can be brought into accord with the rule on some interpretation, therefore the rule cannot guide us. That *would* be absurd. Rather, 'any interpretation still hangs in the air along with what it interprets, and cannot give it any support. Interpretations by themselves do not determine meaning.' Only in a context in which there is an established technique of application of a rule, in which the rule is standardly involved in explanation and justification, in teaching and training, can questions of giving interpretations arise. For only then is the expression *used*, and an internal relation established between act and rule. Only if there *are* genuine rules, only if something does actually count as following (and everything else as going against), is there room for interpreting a rule

---

writing, nor is it any mental accompaniment, therefore there is no 'fact' that constitutes my reading. Therefore, paradoxically, dear reader, reading is logically impossible!

[25] Although not consistently with the meaning of the expression (e.g. 'plus') or with what we understand by it. But that is just what is the question – what does determine meaning?

correctly or incorrectly. And that is established by the existence of a custom, a regular use of the expression of the rule.

Sections 199–200 emphasize that normative behaviour requires a multiplicity of occasions as a context, an evident regularity of point and purpose. §201, removed from its manuscript context, is stripped of any connection with the problem of colour judgment, image-identification, interpreting double-aspect figures. Whereas it originally applied the resolution of the question of §198 to puzzles about recognition, in the course of which it deepened the argument of §198, now its sole role is just the latter. §§198–9 dissolves the question: 'How can a rule determine what counts as accord with it?' by reference to the existence of a normative regularity of conduct. §201 adds a crucial point about understanding a rule (an 'Auffassung' of a rule): 'how one understands a rule need *not* be an interpretation, but may be exhibited in what we call "following the rule" and "going against it" from case to case of its application.'[26] Understanding is mastery of a technique, and how one understands a rule is manifest in the exercise of that technique in practice, in its application to various cases. Far from §201 accepting a paradox and by-passing it by means of a 'sceptical solution', Wittgenstein shows that here, as elsewhere, a paradox is a paradox only in a defective surrounding. If this is remedied the appearance of paradox will vanish.[27] For every paradox is disguised nonsense (and this one is barely even disguised!). Hence it may never be accepted and by-passed by other arguments. It must be dissolved by clarification of concepts.

What has been rejected in §201 is not the truism that rules

---

[26] Our translation. The German reads: 'Dadurch zeigen wir nämlich, daß es eine Auffassung einer Regel gibt, die *nicht* eine *Deutung* ist'. There seems no licence for the translation 'there is a way of grasping (*Erfassen*) a rule'. And 'von Fall zu Fall der Anwendung' seems unhappily rendered by 'in actual cases'.

[27] Cf. Wittgenstein, *Remarks on the Foundations of Mathematics*, ed. G. H. von Wright and G. E. M. Anscombe (Blackwell, Oxford, 1978), p. 410.

guide action (or that we know that our use of an expression conforms with its meaning, or that we are actually applying expressions in accord with their explanations, i.e. the rules for their use). Rather, what is repudiated is the suggestion that a rule determines an action as being in accord with it only in virtue of an interpretation.

The first sentence of §202 merely repeats the penultimate point of §201, viz. how I understand a rule (*meine Auffassung*) is ultimately exhibited not by an interpretation (the substitution of one expression of a rule of another), but in what we call 'following the rule', i.e. in what I do in applying the rule. Hence following a rule is an activity, a *Praxis*. It is a misinterpretation to take '*Praxis*' here to signify a social practice. The contrast here is not between an aria and a chorus, but between looking at a score and singing. The term 'practice' is used here in a similar sense to that in the phrase 'in theory and in practice'. The point is *not* to establish that language necessarily involves a community (see below), but that 'words are deeds'. But a practice is not mere action, it is regular action in accord with a rule, 'not something that happens once, *no matter of what kind*'.[28] Note that nothing in this discussion involves any commitment to a multiplicity of *agents*. All the emphasis is on the regularity, the multiple *occasions*, of action (cf. §199). What is here crucial for Wittgenstein's account of the concept of following a rule is recurrent action in appropriate contexts, action which *counts as* following the rule.[29] Whether others are

---

[28] *Remarks on the Foundations of Mathematics*, p. 335.

[29] It is important to note that Wittgenstein countenances the logical possibility of creatures being born with the ability to speak a language (cf. Wittgenstein, *Philosophical Grammar*, ed. Rush Rhees (Blackwell, Oxford, 1974), p. 188; Wittgenstein, *Blue and Brown Books* (Blackwell, Oxford, 1969), p. 12). *How* one learnt or acquired a language is irrelevant to an account of *what* one has learnt. So if one could be born speaking German, would the absence of speakers of Etruscan be a logical barrier to being born speaking Etruscan? Since Robinson Crusoe could talk to himself, keep a diary, follow rules, would he cease to be able to do so if, unbeknownst to him, the rest of mankind were destroyed by a plague? Obviously not. Is his continuing to be able to do so dependent on the history of his acquisition of

involved is a further question. Of course, with us social creatures rule-following is generally a social practice. But the point of the argument was not to establish this (obvious) fact, but rather to show that rule-following, and hence a language, is a kind of customary behaviour, a form of *action*, not of thought. The 'foundations' of language are not in private experience, the 'given' indefinables, but in normative regularities of conduct.

The remainder of §202, is, in this context, incongruous. For Wittgenstein has not yet explained what following a rule 'privately' means. The passage derives from MS 129, p. 121, where it occurs after the exposition of the private language argument (50 of the 74 remarks constituting the private language argument in the *Investigations* occur in MS 129, only two of them after p. 121). There the allusion to 'following a rule "privately" ' is perspicuously a *back-reference* to the private language argument. By transposition, this remark has become, perhaps inadvertently, an anticipation of §258 (cf. MS 129, p. 43) of the private language argument.

---

his linguistic skills? That seems inconsistent with the principle that 'Teaching as the hypothetical history of our subsequent actions . . . drops out of our considerations' (*Blue and Brown Books*, p. 14).

In MS 165 Wittgenstein imagines a solitary cave-man who uses a picture-language on the walls of his cave. Such a language, he says, would be readily intelligible. Later he imagines a solitary cave-man who speaks only to himself, gives himself orders, etc. Provided he uses simple signs which we could interpret, we could come to understand him. A few pages further on Wittgenstein concludes that to describe the language of a people is to describe a regularity of their behaviour, and to describe a language which someone speaks only to himself is to describe a regularity of *his* behaviour, and not something which can happen only once (cf. MS 129, p. 89).

Of course, we could not *understand* another's language unless we could grasp the rules of his language, follow them as he does, agree with him in the manner of applying them.

4   The private language argument

The foregoing 'archaeological' investigations provide reasons for doubting whether the discussion up till §§201–2 contains the whole of the private language argument proper. We have not *proved* that the core question of the book is not a sceptical one, nor that the solution is not a 'sceptical solution'. But if it is, it does not lie in the passages of §§198–202. Before going on to provide further argument, however, we should look forward from §202 to what is normally conceived as the private language argument in order to see whether Kripke's claims about *it* rest on firmer foundations.

Kripke contends that the 'real private language argument' occurs prior to §243, and that the crucial considerations for that argument are contained in the discussion leading up to §202 which states its conclusions. What is commonly called 'the private language argument' deals with the application of the general conclusions about language drawn in §§138–242 to *the problem of sensations*.[30] Inner experience, like mathematics, allegedly seemed to Wittgenstein to be a counter-example to his view of rules, hence he treats it in detail. The connection between the discussion of sensations and the mathematical reflections is shown in *Remarks on Foundations of Mathematics*, I §3:

> *How do I know* that in working out the series +2 I must write "20004, 20006", and not "20004, 20008"? – (The question: "How do I know that this colour is 'red'?" is similar.)

This passage, Kripke contends,[31] illustrates that Wittgenstein regards the fundamental problems of the philosophy of mathematics and of the private language argument (i.e. the 'problem' of sensation language) as at root identical, stem-

---

[30] Kripke, *Wittgenstein*, p. 79.
[31] Ibid., p. 20.

ming from his paradox. The impossibility of a private language (of sensations) follows from the incorrectness of the private model for language and rules, which is established in §202.

This interpretation of the concerns of §§243ff. is perverse. The private language argument is not about 'the problem of sensations', which constitutes a *prima facie* counter-example to a thesis about rules. It is concerned with establishing the non-primacy of the mental, the 'inner', the subjective. In this enterprise Wittgenstein is stalking a much larger quarry than a potential counter-example to one of his own 'theses' (what theses?), namely the conception of the mental underlying the mainstream of European philosophy since Descartes. It is noteworthy that in his 'Notes for Lectures on "Private Experience" and "Sense Data" ' he worked with the examples of 'seeing red' and 'having a red visual impression' (i.e. perception) no less than with that of toothache (a sensation). And his concern is explicitly with the refutation of idealism and solipsism: the original fly in the fly-bottle is the solipsist![32]

The private language argument is indeed built on the previous discussions, not only of rule-following but also of ostensive definitions, samples, meaning, understanding, and explanation. So too Kant's 'Dialectic' is built on the 'Analytic', but that does not mean that the 'real "Dialectic" ' is the 'Analytic'. What is new in the private language argument is the question of whether a 'private' sample can be employed to give meaning to a word, whether a mental paradigm can be employed, in a stipulation or explanation to oneself, to constitute a norm of correct use.[33] Do the foundations of language

[32] Wittgenstein, 'Notes for Lectures on "Private Experience" and "Sense Data" ', *Phil. Review* 1968, p. 300: 'The solipsist flutters and flutters in the flyglass, strikes against the walls, flutters further. How can he be brought to rest?' Note that in MS 165 Wittgenstein states explcitly that the discussion of a private language *concerns the problems of idealism and solipsism.*

[33] Wittgenstein, ibid.: 'The experience is to serve as a paradigm, and at the same time admittedly it can't be a paradigm.'

lie in mental ostensive definitions of simple 'indefinable' perceptual predicates? Certainly a great tradition of European philosophy embraced such a conception, not only in the remote past, but in the writings of Russell, Carnap (at one stage) and other logical positivists, and indeed, for a brief time, in Wittgenstein's own work.

Nor is it true that the question raised has implicitly been answered by the antecedent discussion of rule-following. After all, it may be argued (and, alas, often is) that given biological nature,[34] you must have just what I have when we both look at tomatoes, hit our shins, etc. So you know what 'pain' or 'looks red' means from your examplar, just as I know from my exemplar. And evolution, or a good angel, has so arranged matters that our exemplars are qualitatively identical. So our public language with its vast network of regularities of action is the confluence, or congruence, of our private languages. So thought and language rest firmly on the bedrock of the subjective.

It is, of course, true that in MSS 129 and 180(a) this argument is ruled out on the grounds that there can be no possibility of establishing an internal relation between a private sample, or 'subjective interpretation', and an action determined in a practice as being in accord with such a 'rule'. Moreover, if something can be a justification for me it must also be capable of functioning as a justification for others. So my 'seeing that this is *so*' cannot function as a justification. There can be no technique of applying a 'private rule'. Such a rule really would 'hang in the air', and there would indeed be no distinction between thinking one is following a rule and

The 'private experience' is a degenerate construction of our grammar (comparable in a sense to tautology and contradiction). And this grammatical monster now fools us; when we wish to do away with it, it seems as though we denied the existence of an experience, say, toothache.

[34] Americans prefer the terminology of the computer age – so: given that we are all 'wired-up' in the same way!

actually following it. Here one would have only a *'Schein-Praxis'* (paradigmatically exemplified by the illusory consulting of a private table in the imagination (MS 180(a), 59)). But the argument to establish these conclusions *is* the private language argument! By transposing §202 from the vicinity of §§377–81 it has been deprived of its argumentative support. As it stands, the last sentence does indeed state *a* conclusion of the private language argument, but now *it* 'hangs in the air'.

Even if we follow Kripke's interpretation, nothing significant is altered. 'Any individual who claims to have mastered the concept of . . . will be judged by a community to have done so if his particular responses agree with those of the community in enough cases, especially the simple ones . . .'[35] So we may accept, e.g. that we need community support to indulge in, say, colour predication (or any other concept-using game), but given that we agree in judgments, agreement in private definitions is ensured (by a good angel; or the 'argument to the best explanation'). Hence it is not the case that the conclusion of the private language argument has been proven before it is raised in §§243ff.

It is no less misleading to point at *Remarks on the Foundations of Mathematics* I §3 to establish a connection between considerations of rule-following and the private language argument

---

[35] Kripke, *Wittgenstein*, pp. 91f. In effect Kripke's interpretation of §202 assigns a meaning to the word 'privately' which is at odds with Wittgenstein's use of the term. Kripke holds that someone would follow a rule 'privately' if his actions are considered in isolation from the behaviour of his community in respect of responses to this rule. But on Wittgenstein's account it is essential that the putative rule allegedly being followed 'privately' is one to the *expression* of which only *I* have access, i.e. it is expressed by a private ostensive definition. Hence it is, for a quite different reason from Kripke's, *impossible* for another to ascertain whether or not my applications of this 'rule' are correct. Kripke's objection to private ostensive definitions must be that the attempt to apply any such rule must leave the agent stranded, as it were, *ex officio*, on his own desert island. But this leaves open the possibility that all agents are stranded on the *same* island (that public language is a congruence of private languages built separately on private ostensive definitions).

proper. *Of course* there are deep affinities between questions in philosophy of mathematics and questions in philosophy of mind. But this passage does *not* point to one. Here there is a connection between expanding the series '+2', and applying the predicate 'red'. But the concern of the private language argument is not with *objective* predications, but with *subjective* ones. Wittgenstein states that the question 'How do I know this colour is "red"?' is similar to the arithmetical question, not that the question 'How do I know that this experience is "seeing red"?' is similar. In fact the two pairs of question are very different. In the first two cases we are concerned with the bedrock of rules. No further rule mediates between the rule 'Add 2' and saying '20004, 20006', or between an ostensive definition of 'red' and a judgment that this is red. But the private language argument focuses on the case of 'I am in pain' or 'I am seeing red', where the issue is not bridging the 'gulf' between a genuine rule (an ostensive definition) and its use or application but whether there is any such thing as a bogus 'private' rule, viz, a *private* ostensive definition. The argument turns on such matters as the first-/third-person asymmetry of psychological predicates, criterionless self-ascription and behavioural criteria for third-person ascription, the non-cognitive status of avowals, etc.

Finally, it is misleading to represent the *Remarks on the Foundations of Mathematics* as an examination of an apparent counter-example to the discussion of rules (as the private language argument examines sensations) – on the contrary, the discussion of rules, of rule-following and of application of rules is used to shed light upon central questions of the philosophy of mathematics, viz. the nature of mathematical necessity, the status of proof, and the relation of mathematics to logic.

5   Kripke's sceptical problem

So far we have compared Kripke's discussion to Wittgenstein's, and found *prima facie* reasons for hesitating to embrace his interpretation. We now turn to an examination of the cogency of some of his arguments.

Kripke casts the central problem of the *Investigations* in terms of a 'sceptical hypothesis about a change in my usage'.[36] How can I know that my understanding of 'W', what I mean by 'W', determines the correctness of applying 'W' to *this*? The sceptic doubts whether any instruction I gave myself in the past compels or justifies this answer (rather than an absurd one). Kripke in effect shifts Wittgenstein's problem of how, in what sense, a rule determines its application, to a problem of the relation between my past and present intentions, my meaning addition by 'plus' (and not a different arithmetical operation christened 'quaddition').

This shift is one from an altogether natural belief to a bizarre one. For it is natural to think that given that e.g. 'red' or 'plus' means what it does, it *follows* that *this* is red, or that $68 + 57 = 125$. But it is not plausible, still less obvious, that in answering the questions 'What colour is this?' or 'What is $68 + 57$?' one conceives of oneself as following an instruction that one gave oneself in the past. *A fortiori* in remarking 'that is a splendid red' (looking at a field of poppies), one does not conceive oneself as obeying one's past instructions about the meaning of 'red', as opposed to using the word 'red' in accord with its meaning.[37]

Why does Kripke's predicament lead first to scepticism and ultimately to conceptual nihilism? The reason offered is that we are naturally inclined to say that we 'know, directly, and with a fair degree of certainty'[38] that we mean W by 'W'. But Wittgenstein shows that no mental event, act, activity or

---

[36] Ibid., p. 13.

[37] The plausibility of this bizarre picture seems to turn on the now popular conception of language as quasi-contractual, as if the distinction between correct and incorrect use of an expression turned on 'keeping faith' with one's past undertakings. This seems as misguided as the now derided conviction that a social contract would provide the only possible foundation for political liberties, rights, and duties.

[38] Kripke, *Wittgenstein*, p. 40.

process which may occur when we mean or understand something constitutes the meaning or understanding. This leaves
us, apparently, only one move, viz. to claim that meaning
W by 'W' is an irreducible experience known directly by
introspection. Against this Wittgenstein argues at length, and
persuasively. We might try a last stand, contending that meaning is a primitive, *sui generis*, state:

> Such a move may in a sense be irrefutable, and taken in
> an appropriate way Wittgenstein may even accept it. But
> it seems desperate: it leaves the nature of this postulated
> primitive state . . . completely mysterious. It is not
> supposed to be an introspectible state, yet we supposedly
> are aware of it with some fair degree of certainty when-
> ever it occurs. For how else can each of us be confident
> that he *does*, at present, mean addition by 'plus'? Even
> more important is the logical difficulty implicit in
> Wittgenstein's sceptical argument. I think that
> Wittgenstein argues, not merely as we have said hitherto,
> that introspection shows that the alleged 'qualitative'
> state of understanding is a chimera, but also that it is
> logically impossible (or at least that there is a considerable
> logical difficulty) for there to be a state of 'meaning
> addition by "plus" ' at all.[39]

This reasoning betokens misunderstandings of Wittgenstein's
argument. Hence we will interrupt exposition of Kripke's
sceptical problem to show where it went off Wittgenstein's
rails.

First, according to Wittgenstein, 'I know that I mean . . .' is
either an emphatic manner of saying that I mean such-and-
such or it is nonsense.[40] There is no distinction between my

[39] Ibid., pp. 51f.
[40] It could also be an oblique way of explaining that the expression of
uncertainty here is senseless, as in 'Either I mean red by "red" or something
else, I'm not sure'. Cf. *Philosophical Investigations*, §§246–7.

meaning W by 'W' and my knowing that I mean W by 'W' (unlike, say, my knowing that A is dead and A's being dead). So there is no question here of 'knowing with a fair degree of certainty' or of 'knowing directly'. My (appropriately) confident assertion that I mean addition by 'plus' does not rest on evidence of any kind.

Second, according to Wittgenstein, meaning and intending are not experiences at all, *a fortiori* not irreducible experiences known introspectively. But it does not follow at all, nor did Wittgenstein suggest that it followed, that I do not mean or intend the things I take myself to mean to intend, the things I sincerely say that I mean or intend.[41] All that follows is that this philosophical picture of meaning and intending, of self-knowledge and privileged access, is wrong. What Wittgenstein is concerned with is not scepticism about our right to say that we mean this or that, that we intend so-and-so, but extirpation of philosophical confusion.

Third, Wittgenstein does not argue that introspection, i.e. an 'experimental method', reveals that as a matter of fact there is no 'primitive state' of understanding. He does indeed argue that it is logically impossible for there to be a *state* of meaning W by 'W', but not in the manner Kripke suggests. And *this* argument does not even *suggest* that I do not mean what I normally say that I mean. The argument is that understanding, meaning and intending are not *states* of any kind.[42] Mental states are such things as being nervous, excited, exhilarated. These obtain for a time and can be clocked, interrupted and resumed. They run a course, are subject to degrees of intensity and lapse during sleep. Not so are understanding, meaning and intending. But it does not follow, according to Wittgenstein, that one does not mean addition by 'plus', or that one does not intend to play chess when one sincerely says 'Let's play chess'.

[41] There is, in certain contexts of 'mean' or 'intend', a problem about self-deception. The present context is not such a one.

[42] For detailed discussion, see Baker and Hacker, *Wittgenstein: Understanding and Meaning*, pp. 595ff.

Fourth, even if, *per impossibile*, meaning *were* a state, this would not solve Wittgenstein's problem. For how could any *state* bridge the apparent gap, the logical gulf, between a rule and its application? What feature of a 'state of meaning' could make it right to apply the rule thus or otherwise? Is it not obvious that this hypothetical state of meaning would be tantamount to another interpretation of the rule? The jump to its application would still have to be made.

Of course, according to Wittgenstein, I may confidently say that I mean addition by 'plus', but not because I am intro-spectively aware of my inner state of meaning. Rather, as I am confident that I intend to play chess (and not some other game), or confident that what I now expect is John to come (and not, John to go, James to come or the pound sterling to fluctuate). If my confidence rested on an inner awareness, it would be inductive. I would have to reason that whenever I have in the past had this inner state, then I have gone on to . . . But then I ought to say 'I think I intend to play chess. Let's see!' which is absurd.

With these rectifications behind us, let us resume exposition of Kripke. The claim that there is no such thing as the 'state of meaning addition by "plus" ' leads directly to the culmination of his sceptical argument. The sceptic holds, Kripke claims, 'that no fact about my past history – nothing that was ever in my mind, or in my external behavior – establishes that I meant plus rather than quus'[43] and, in view of the introspective argument, 'it appears to follow that there was no *fact* about me that constituted my having meant plus'.[44] This argument, in particular its phrasing in terms of *facts*, is crucial for Kripke's interpretation. For, he claims, the target of *Investigations* §§1– 133 is the truth-conditional theory of meaning as propounded in the *Tractatus*. According to that theory, what makes pro-positions true are corresponding facts-in-the-world (hence what would make 'I mean W by "W" ' true would be some fact-in-my-mind). And what gives sentences their meaning

[43] Kripke, *Wittgenstein*, p. 13.
[44] Ibid., p. 21.

are their correlations with possible facts or conditions in the world, viz. their truth-conditions.[45] The repudiation of this truth-conditional theory of meaning is the pivotal point of Wittgenstein's alleged 'Sceptical Solution' to his alleged sceptical problem. He is held to agree with the sceptic that there is no fact-in-the-world that constitutes my meaning W by 'W', but also to repudiate the truth-conditional theory of meaning that requires the obtaining of such facts to make true claims about meaning.

This is off-target. It misinterprets the *Tractatus* conception of truth-conditions (see below). It distorts the structure of the argument of the *Investigations*. And, by Wittgenstein's lights, it is plainly wrong.

First, *no* facts are *in* the world. It is a fact that Oxford is in England, but that fact is not in England, nor yet in France – for facts are not in space. Nor are they temporal entities: the fact that Hastings was fought in 1066 did not occur in 1066, since it is Hastings – the battle – that occurred then, not the fact. The fact that it occurred in 1066 did not cease to be a fact in 1067, nor was it a mere proto-fact in the womb of History in 1065. Hence the fact that I yesterday meant W by 'W' is not a fact-that-was-in-the-world-yesterday. And the fact that I now mean W by 'W' is not a fact-in-my-mind-now. But if I did mean W by 'W', then it *is* a fact that I so meant, and if I now mean W by 'W' then it is a fact that I so mean.

Second, if Kripke wishes, one *can* say that the fact about me that constituted my having meant addition by 'plus' is the fact that I so meant. For if I *did* so mean, it is a fact that I so meant (and I will tell you if you ask me). Of course, the stick won't move. But that is because one has got hold of the wrong end of it.

Third, to be sure, when I tell you that I meant W by 'W', or that I meant you to go '1002, 1004' or that I intend to visit London tomorrow, I do not read these statements off the 'facts-in-the-world'. Kripke intimates that Wittgenstein's only alternative to the 'Sceptical Solution' is a picture according to which my confidently saying what I mean must result from my reading off what I mean from a fact-in-the-world (in my mind). This is precisely what Wittgenstein denies. The picture of facts-in-the-world is a muddle. Its solution does not consist in denying that there are any facts concerning my meaning things by words, but in sorting out the muddle.

Fourth, if the repudiation of his earlier truth-conditional theory of meaning (understood as involving correspondence with facts-in-the-world) is *the* key issue in *Investigations* §§1–133 and is crucial to the solution of the sceptical paradox, it cannot but be surprising that Wittgenstein has *no* discussion of facts in the whole book. Nowhere does he examine the concept of a fact, nor suggest that it is not facts that make propositions true. Is this because he had nothing to say? Or because he was so cagey?

As a matter of fact, Wittgenstein had a very straightforward way with facts – and stated it clearly in what is now published as *Philosophical Grammar*.[46] That he did not incorporate these remarks into the *Investigations* strongly suggests that he was not aiming at this target at all. His moves are simple. He does not deny that what makes the proposition that *p* true is the fact that *p*. He does not repudiate the claim that the proposition determines in advance what will make it true (what fact must obtain to make it true). Rather he rejects the metaphysical picture that goes with these claims. For these are grammatical statements, not metaphysical profundities. They concern intra-linguistic articulations, not the ultimate connections between language and reality. It is a convention of grammar that 'The proposition that *p*' = 'The proposition that the fact that *p* makes true'. And so too 'The fact that *p*' = 'The fact that makes the proposition that *p* true'. Like everything meta-physical the harmony between thought and reality is to be found *in the grammar of the language*.[47]

[46]   Wittgenstein, *Philosophical Grammar*, pp. 161f., 199ff., 212ff.

[47]   For a more detailed analysis of Wittgenstein's resolution of the problem of the pictoriality of thought, see P. M. S. Hacker, 'The Rise and Fall of the Picture Theory', in *Perspectives on the Philosophy of Wittgenstein*, ed. I. Block.

Finally, it is noteworthy that the way Kripke sets up his sceptical paradox initially parallels traditional scepticism in assuming that only entailment will license a derivative cognitive claim. Nothing in the past or in the present, in my mind or my behaviour, *entails* that I now mean by 'plus' what I previously meant by 'plus'. And so on. This observation parallels defences of scepticism about the past, about other minds or about induction. And, of course, we need not accept any such arguments. What shows that I meant green by 'green' is the way I explained 'green', and what shows that I meant grue is giving a quite different explanation. That I gave such-and-such an explanation does not *entail* that in applying 'green' to this object I am using 'green' in accord with what I meant by it hitherto, but it provides perfectly adequate grounds for that judgment (if anyone is interested in such a bizarre question). How I use an expression, how I explain an expression, how I use the explanation as a norm of correctness (in indefinitely many cases, new and old), what I *count* as applying the expression in accord with its explanation (its meaning) shows what I understand by it. *This* sceptical problem can be side-stepped. But we may doubt whether *this* was ever Wittgenstein's problem!

6 Kripke's sceptical solution

Initial scepticism, according to Kripke, leads us to doubt whether we are applying words in accord with how we have in the past meant them. This led, by a quick route, to conceptual nihilism which denies that there is any such thing as meaning, and faces us with a paradox: language is impossible. Wittgenstein's solution, Kripke claims, consists in rejecting a truth-conditional theory of meaning in favour of assertion-conditions. Within this framework of thought, he can accept the sceptic's premises that there is no fact-in-the-world constituting my meaning plus by 'plus', hence (*sic*!) that 'Jones means plus by "plus" ' has no truth-conditions,[48] yet deny the sceptic's paradox. What he does is to describe the assertion-conditions of such statements, viz.:

> *Jones* is entitled, subject to correction by others, pro-visionally to say, "I mean addition by 'plus'," whenever he has the feeling of confidence – "now I can go on!" – that he can give 'correct' responses in new cases; and *he* is entitled, again provisionally and subject to correction by others, to judge a new response to be 'correct' simply because it is the response he is inclined to give. . . . *Smith* will judge Jones to mean addition by 'plus' only if he judges that Jones's answers to particular addition problems agree with those *he* is inclined to give . . .
> . . . Any individual who claims to have mastered the concept of addition will be judged by the community to have done so if his particular responses agree with those of the community in enough cases . . .[49]

It is difficult here to find any similitude to Wittgenstein's arguments. Indeed, it is difficult to see *any* plausibility in the argument, irrespective of whether it is Wittgenstein's.

We are asked to accept as plausible the following exchange: we ask Jones 'Do you mean addition by "plus" (or red by "red", bachelor by "bachelor", etc.)?' And he is then supposed to answer: 'Yes, I do, and I know that I do because I feel confident I can answer such questions as "What is 68 + 57?" correctly (or "What colour is this?", or "Is John a bachelor?").' But this is bizarre. That one feels confident is not what *entitles* one to say that one means W by 'W'. And that one is *inclined* to answer thus-and-so is not what *entitles* one to judge one's answer to be correct.[50]

---

[48] Cf. Kripke, *Wittgenstein*, p. 86.
[49] Ibid., pp. 90ff.
[50] It is curious that Kripke carefully encloses 'correct' with scare-quotes. Is it that there is no such thing as correctly using a sign on this account? The only option Kripke has *explicitly* left open is a Platonist one, viz. it is in the

First, other things being equal, I will *always* claim to mean W by 'W'. The question is *what* I mean by 'W', i.e. whether I actually understand this word, whether I know what it means. The issue is not whether I am now using it in accord with what I previously meant by it, but whether I am now using it in accord with its meaning. The answer to these various questions is *not* to insist on my confidence, but to say what I mean, i.e. to explain what 'W' means; e.g. that 'bachelor' means an unmarried male, 'red' means this colour (pointing at a ripe tomato), and 'plus' means that function which when 2 and 3 are its arguments, yields 5 as its value, and which, when. . . . Of course, these explanations do not bridge the gap between meaning and use, rule and application. But no explanation of any kind could do that, since the 'gap' is categorial. But giving these explanations *does*, *ceteris paribus*, provide adequate grounds for judging what a person means, and whether he knows what an expression means.

Second, the very idea that I could have an *entitlement* to say 'I mean W by "W" ' is odd insofar as it implies that there are grounds, assertability conditions, the obtaining of which I must establish before I may say that I mean such-and-such. But there are no more grounds for *my* saying 'I mean W by "W" ' than there are grounds, assertability conditions, for saying 'I intend to go to London tomorrow' or 'I want a drink'. So too, it is misleading to suggest that there is here a question of my *knowing* that I mean W by "W" (viz. if I have a title to assert, then *ceteris paribus*, I know . . .). But 'I know that I mean W by "W" ' is just an emphatic insistence that I do mean W by "W".

Kripke's description of the assertion-conditions for a third-person ascription is no less strange. We must imagine the following exchange: we ask Smith, 'Does Jones mean addition

_____

nature of such-and-such mathematical object to yield such-and-such a value for such-and-such arguments (cf. Kripke, *Wittgenstein*, pp. 53f.). But this is certainly not Wittgenstein's view. And Kripke does not explain what he thinks Wittgenstein's view is.

by "plus"?' He replies, 'Yes, because whenever he is asked "What are *a* plus *b*?" (for any *a* and *b*), he always gives the same answer as I give'. This is awry.

First, whether Jones gives the same answer as Smith is beside the point. The question is whether he gives the correct answer,[51] i.e. what *counts*, in such a case, as the correct answer. In some cases, even this procedure would be absurd. For example, does Jones mean bachelor by 'bachelor'? Are we to say: 'Yes, whenever he is asked whether Mr A is a bachelor he gives the same answer I am inclined to give'? But in most cases the answer I would be inclined to give would be 'I don't know'! Would this response satisfy the assertion conditions for 'Jones means bachelor by "bachelor"'?

Second, the analysis seems to suggest that Smith cannot judge that Jones understands 'W' (means W by 'W') unless (a) he knows how Jones applies 'W' to new instances, and (b) he takes a given application of 'W' to be correct simply because it is the one he himself is inclined to give. But it is a conceptual truth that I am entitled to judge someone to mean W by 'W' (to understand 'W') on the grounds of the *explanations* of 'W' he gives. If he says 'By "bachelor" I mean an unmarried man', is that not *enough*? *Must* he answer the question of whether Genghis Khan at the age of 22 was a bachelor? And must he answer it the way *I* am inclined to?[52]

Putting together the first- and third-person assertion-

---

[51] Or at least, in the arithmetical case, that he goes through the correct procedure.

[52] To this the reply might be that the requirement is not merely that he gives the same reply I am inclined to give, but rather that given the same information, he gives the same reply. So given that he knows that Genghis Khan was an unmarried man at the age of 22, he would answer the question of whether he was a bachelor in the same way as I am inclined to, given that information. This may be conceded; of course he will give the same answer – because he knows (as I do) what 'bachelor' means. It is nor our agreement that is the ground for the judgment that he means bachelor by 'bachelor', but rather the explanation of its meaning which he gives and the applications of the word that he makes. The agreement is a framework condition for the language-game (*infra* p. 45), not part of the rules of the game.

conditions as a general account, two points still stand forth as baffling. First, truth-conditions were meant to provide an account of the meanings of sentences. Giving the truth-conditions is generally supposed to be a way of giving or explaining the meaning of a sentence. Assertion-conditions are presumably to inherit this role from truth-conditions in Kripke's account. So the *meaning* of 'A means addition (or whatever) by "plus" (or whatever)' is supposed to be *given* by Kripke's specification of its assertion-conditions. But would *anyone* thus explain what 'A means W by "W"' means to someone who genuinely wanted to know? And would such an explanation provide a norm for the correct use of 'means'?

Second, has the original sceptical question really been answered? The problem was set up by arguing that we can never have adequate *grounds* to judge that anyone now uses an expression in accord with its previous meaning (with what he, or we, previously meant by it). The sceptical solution is that no fact about past or present can tell us that our current use coheres with our past use. But if we all share common inclinations to apply the term thus-and-so, then we all now mean W by 'W', or, more carefully, as long as a speaker does *not* apply 'W' differently from the way the rest of the community is inclined to apply it, then he will be accepted as following the rule for 'W', as meaning by 'W' what everyone else means.

But does this really resolve the sceptical question? Given that no one previously ever added 57 and 68, how do we know that our present community-wide inclination to answer '125' accords with what we previously meant by 'plus', i.e. with what we would have been inclined to say, had we previously been asked what 57 + 68 is? Like Kripke, we put the challenge 'in terms of a sceptical hypothesis about a change in [our] usage'.[53] For there was yesterday no *satisfied* assertion-condition for our meaning either plus or quus, since we had no inclination to answer '57 + 68' either way, as the question, *ex hypothesi*, had never occurred to anyone hitherto.

[53] Parallel to Kripke, *Wittgenstein*, p. 13.

7   Robinson Crusoe rides again

Kripke's assertion-conditions account is part of his picture of
Wittgenstein's argument, but not the whole. In addition, he
contends, Wittgenstein describes the role and utility in our
lives of assertions that someone means such-and-such by his
words, or that his present use of a word accords with what he
previously meant by it. It turns out, however, that this role
and the conditions of assertion are inapplicable to a single
person considered in isolation.[54] If one person is considered in
isolation, the notion of his following a rule can have *no* substantive content. For as long as we regard him as following a
rule 'privately', i.e. merely following his inclinations (*sic*!),
then there is no difference between his thinking he is following
a rule and his following one. It is *this* argument which, by
§202, rules out as incoherent the private language which is
introduced only in §§243ff.

What then of Robinson Crusoe on his desert island? It does
not follow, Kripke claims, that he cannot be said to follow
rules. 'What does follow is that *if* we think of Crusoe as
following rules, we are taking him into our community and
applying our criteria for rule following to him. The falsity of
the private model need not mean that a *physically isolated*
individual cannot be said to follow rules; rather that an
individual, *considered in isolation* (whether or not he is physically isolated), cannot be said to do so.'[55]

---

[54] Ibid., pp. 79, 89.

[55] Ibid., p. 110.; a similar bizarre view is expressed by C. Peacocke in his
defence of what he calls 'The community view' of rules: 'The community
view can count such a person [as Crusoe] as a genuine rule-follower if he
reacts to new examples in the same way as would members of our community, or of some other conceivable community.' See C. Peacocke,
'Reply: Rule-following: the Nature of Wittgenstein's Arguments', in
Wittgenstein: to follow a rule, ed. S. Holtzman and C. Leich (Routledge and
Kegan Paul, London, 1981), pp. 93f. Note that the subjunctive, together
with the requirement of mere *conceivability* of a community, robs the
qualification of any restrictive content whatever.

This is muddled. In the first place, it is quite wrong to suppose that distinctions between appearance and reality are inapplicable to an individual in isolation, or are ones which that individual cannot employ. In the particular case of rule-following, there is no reason why Crusoe should not follow a pattern or paradigm, making occasional mistakes perhaps, and occasionally (but maybe not always) noticing and correcting his mistakes. That he is following a rule will show itself in the manner in which he uses the formulation of the rule as a canon or norm of correctness. Hence, to take a simple example, he might use the pattern – – – . . . – – – . . . as a rule or pattern to follow in decorating the walls of his house; when he notices four dots in a sequence he manifests annoyance with himself. He goes back and rubs one out, and perhaps checks carefully adjacent marks, comparing them with his 'master-pattern'. And so on. Of course, he is *not* merely following his 'inclinations',[56] but rather following the rule. And it is his behaviour, including his corrective behaviour, which shows both that he is following the rule, and *what he counts as following the rule*.

It might be asked how an unseen observer of such solitary rule-following could distinguish Crusoe's making a mistake from his following a more complex pattern, and his following a more complex pattern from his non-normative behaviour. How could one justify the claim that the solitary man is either following or breaking a rule at all? The answer is that if one must, *ex hypothesi*, remain unseen, it will be very difficult to understand him. If the rules are simple, we might guess aright. If they are complex, we might not. Reflect that if we observed the self-addressed speech of a shipwrecked monolingual Tibetan, our chances of coming to understand him are remote.

[56] There is something very wrong about recent talk of 'following one's inclinations' when applying rules. We do *not* teach children arithmetic by teaching them to follow their *inclinations*. We do not even teach them to have the same *inclinations* as we have. We teach them to follow arithmetical *rules*, we teach them that getting such-and-such results is what *counts* as following this or that rule. When we hit bedrock we do indeed follow the rule blindly, but that is not to say that we follow our inclinations blindly!

But he surely could talk to himself, keep a diary, give orders to himself, play Tibetan solitaire. Once the restriction of *unseen* observation is lifted, however, matters change altogether. Gestures ('the natural language of mankind' as Augustine says), common human nature, and *interaction with* the castaway provide the necessary leverage. Of course, to understand him we must grasp his rules. Whether we are succeeding in doing so is something we shall see from the extent to which *our* attempts to follow *his* rules are in agreement with his behaviour. But whether he is following a rule is independent of whether anyone else is actually doing so too.

Second, Kripke rightly concedes that Crusoe may follow rules, but insists that in saying of him that he does, we 'are taking him into our community and applying our criteria for rule following to him'. This seems confused. This 'taking him into our community' will do little to alleviate Crusoe's solitude. What is it supposed to mean? Does it mean that in saying that he is following a rule we are applying our criteria for rule-following to him? Well – are there other criteria? This, presumably, is what 'rule-following' *means*. When we say of the cat that it is hunting the mouse, we are applying our criteria of hunting to it. Do we thereby take the cat into our community? This, it might be replied, is beside the point. That we 'take him into our community' consists in the fact that we judge that he is following a rule only if he satisfies the assertion-conditions of following a rule, and *these*, Kripke contends, stipulate that A can be said to mean W by 'W', to follow such-and-such a rule, if he applies the rule (uses 'W') as other members of the community do, if his responses and inclinations agree with theirs. Since Crusoe is not a member of any community, in judging him to be following a rule, we must be 'taking him into our community', judging his responses to agree with ours.

Must we? Must Crusoe's rules be the same as ours? Must his colour vocabulary be isomorphic with ours? Could he not invent new rules, play new games? To be sure, in order to *grasp* them, we must understand what counts, in Crusoe's *practice*, as following the rules. And that must be evident in Crusoe's *activities*. But that is not the same as checking to see whether his responses agree with ours, let alone a matter of 'taking him into our community'. And our judgment that he is following his rules is quite independent of any judgment about how most members of the English-Speaking Peoples would react. Indeed, given Kripke's rule-scepticism, how are we supposed to *know* how our community *would* react, given that the rule is novel, or is being applied to a novel circumstance?

Interestingly, Wittgenstein did explicitly discuss Robinson Crusoe in his notebooks. MS 124 has an early version of *Investigations* §243(a), a discussion of the imaginary mono-loguists, whose language is translatable by the explorer. Couldn't we imagine people who speak only to themselves? In that case, Wittgenstein responds, each person could have his own language. There could be men who know only language-games that one plays by oneself, viz. ordering oneself, telling oneself, asking and answering oneself, etc. How they learnt their language is here irrelevant, he adds. An explorer who observed the behaviour of such monologuists could translate their languages. Later Wittgenstein remarks that the private language that he has described above is one which Robinson could have spoken to himself on his island. If anyone had observed him, he could have learnt this language. For the meanings of the words of his (contingently) private language are shown in Robinson's *behaviour*. [57]

There is no hint here that in attributing rule-following to Crusoe, in judging him to mean such-and-such by what he says, we are 'taking him into our community'. There is no suggestion that our concept of rule-following or of meaning is

[57] Cf. MS 124, pp. 213 and 221. A similar discussion of the language of Robinson Crusoe 'considered in isolation' occurs in MS 116, 117, where Wittgenstein examines a distinction between subjective and objective under-standing. Crusoe could certainly play language-games by himself, Wittgenstein remarks. If one secretly observed his sign-using activities, and if one discerned in them certain kinds of complex regularities, one would rightly judge him to be using a language of his own.

limited to *our* rules, or to what *we* mean by signs. There is no claim that his responses must agree with ours (he may have invented a new branch of mathematics; he may employ a different colour geometry from ours; or he may apply names of notes immediately, given that he has perfect pitch). The claim does not involve insistence on community-aid for solitary rule-followers, but on *regularities* of action of sufficient *complexity* to yield normativity. The criteria for whether Crusoe is following a rule do indeed lie in his behaviour, but not in his behaviour agreeing with independent hypothetical or counterfactual behaviour of ours.

It is noteworthy that immediately following the last remark about Crusoe in MS 124, Wittgenstein introduces the real private language argument, i.e. a draft of *Investigations* §243(b). There is no hint that he considers such a language to have been ruled out by his antecedent reflections on rule-following in general or on Crusoe's solitary rule-following in particular.

8 Further diagnosis

The discussion thus far suggests that Kripke has misinterpreted Wittgenstein's argument 'in the Large and in the Small'. Three substantial misunderstandings or distortions ramify throughout his essay. These are likely to mislead readers and to lead to futile debates about Wittgenstein's intentions. The following observations may help to avoid this.

(i) Kripke sets up his sceptical problem (the 'real private language argument') in terms of what a speaker means by an expression, of whether he is now using an expression in accord with what he previously meant by it. This is a highly misleading way of broaching the core problem Wittgenstein is concerned with, namely, what is involved in a speaker's understanding an expression, knowing what it means, using it in accord with a correct explanation of its meaning. Kripke's strategy is misleading because it runs together the internally related, but distinct, notions of what an expression means and understanding an expression. Focusing on the issue of conformity of current use with a pattern of past use conflates the question of the persistence of understanding (an ability) with the question of the correctness of the present use (conformity with a norm). Kripke vainly attempts to extricate himself from the consequent muddle by invoking community aid. Wittgenstein's strategy is entirely different. He is careful to keep these questions distinct. He correlates understanding both with the use of an expression and with explaining its meaning, and he stresses that these correlations must not be conflated. Since meaning is a correlate of understanding, the meaning of a word is also linked both with its use and with explanations of its meaning. The meaning of a word *is* what is explained by an explanation of its meaning. And it is also the manner in which the word is used in speech. Understanding the meaning of a word is akin to an ability; it is the mastery of a technique of using a symbol according to rules. The criteria of understanding lie in behaviour, in the use of the expression in accord with (in what *counts* as accord with) its explanation, the rules for its use, and in the giving of correct explanations of its meaning (which may be by example, paraphrase, contextual paraphrase, ostension, *Merkmal*-definition, etc.). Not only agreement in judgments, as Kripke suggests, but also agreement in definitions is essential to meaning and understanding – and the notions must be described with sufficient subtlety that logic is not thereby abolished. It is unclear whether Kripke satisfies this obvious requirement. On p. 111 he claims, following Wittgenstein, that truth is not to be equated with what most people hold to be true. He insists that Wittgenstein has no theory of truth-conditions, necessary and sufficient conditions for the correctness of one response rather than another to a new addition problem (and, presumably, to a new colour predication). Wittgenstein's assertability conditions story, according to Kripke, does not say that the correct answer to an addition problem is the one everyone gives, but only the platitude that if everyone agrees upon a certain answer, then no one will feel justified in calling that answer wrong. But *is* the answer right? What does it *mean*, according to this story, for an answer to be right as opposed to wrong? Unless an answer *is* forthcoming, Kripke's Wittgenstein, unlike the author of the *Philosophical Investigations*, will have abolished logic!

(ii) The role of *agreement* is certainly paramount in Wittgenstein's argument. My use of an expression must agree, accord, with my correct explanation of what it means. If I explain 'red' by pointing at a sample, saying 'This is red', then when I judge an object A to be red, A must be *this* (pointing at the sample) colour. Moreover, *ceteris paribus*, my current use of an expression must agree with my previous use. I must lay down the yardstick alongside reality *in the same way*, i.e. in what is called 'the same way' from occasion to occasion. And reality must be sufficiently stable so that the yardstick typically gives the same result when the same object is measured on successive occasions. Otherwise measurement in particular and the application of concepts to reality in general become pointless. Finally, the 'language-games' I engage in with others can be played only if we agree in explanations (definitions) and also, by and large, agree in applications (judgments).

Kripke appreciates the centrality of the notion of agreement for Wittgenstein, but distorts its function. We noted that he allots no significant role to agreement in definitions (explanations) and has nothing to say on the relationship between agreement in judgments and agreement in definitions. However, it also seems to be the case that Kripke's Wittgenstein conceives of agreement as *constitutive* of my meaning W by 'W'. Someone is judged by the community to have mastered such-and-such a concept 'if his particular responses agree with those of the community in enough cases'.[58] Someone in a community is said to follow a rule 'as long as he agrees in his responses with the . . . responses produced by the members of *that* community'.[59] On this account, agreement with a com-

---

[58] Kripke, *Wittgenstein*, p. 92.
[59] Ibid., p. 96.

munity is part of the assertion-conditions of 'meaning W by
"W" ' and hence part of its meaning. Is this Wittgenstein's
view?

For Wittgenstein, agreement is a framework condition for
the existence of language-games, but is *not* constitutive of any
game. Hence it is not part of the criteria for whether A *understands* 'plus' or 'red'. These are, rather, that A explains correctly what the expressions mean, and typically uses them
correctly. That A understands what 'red' means is shown by
his giving a correct explanation (ostensive definition) of 'red',
as well as by his saying of my red rose 'That is red'. That others
would also characterize my rose as red is not part of the criteria
for A's understanding, knowing the meaning of 'red'. But the
framework for these concept-exercising activities *is* general
agreement.[60] Similarly Wittgenstein contends that proofs in
mathematics stand in need of ratification, and in the absence of
a consensus in ratifications, mathematicians would not come
to any understanding, and the concept of calculation would
have no application.[61] But this is not to say that it is agreement
in ratification that *makes* such-and-such operations calculation.
Far from it, 'the agreement of ratifications is the precondition
of our language-game, it is not affirmed in it'. The subject
of agreement in judgments and definitions is treated by
Wittgenstein with great subtlety. We shall not try here to
unravel its complexities. But it is clear that he does not conceive of agreement in judgments as a constitutive element of a
language-game.

Kripke does not take sufficiently seriously Wittgenstein's
insistence that 'Following according to the rule is FUNDA-
MENTAL to our language-game. It characterizes what we
call description.'[62] He apparently wants to go *behind* rule-
following to agreement. But there is nothing behind:

[60] See Wittgenstein, *Remarks on the Foundations of Mathematics*, p. 323:
'peaceful agreement . . . belongs to the framework out of which our
language works'. Cf. *Philosophical Investigations*, §240.
[61] Wittgenstein, *Remarks on the Foundations of Mathematics*, p. 365.
[62] Ibid., p. 330.

It is no use, for example, going back to the concept of agreement, because it is no more certain that one proceeding is in agreement with another, than that it has happened in accordance with a rule. Admittedly, going according to a rule is also founded on agreement.[63]

It is not surprising that if one tries to go beyond rule-following into the framework that makes it possible, one will, in the process, lose the very concept of normativity one is trying to clarify; and with it too the distinction between correct and incorrect.

What a teacher teaches a child is not to have the same inclinations others have, but to follow a rule correctly. The learner must learn to use the rule, the explanation of meaning, as a standard of correct use. He must learn to see such-and-such results as criteria for following the rule correctly. And all this takes place within the background context of a (shared) practice of using the rule in this way. If the learner is to master shared concepts he must learn what *counts* as following the rule. And

> what the correct following of a rule consists in cannot be described *more closely* than by describing the *learning* of 'proceeding according to the rule'. And this description is an everyday one, like that of cooking and sewing, for example.[64]

What counts as correct is not the response we are inclined to give. The learner is *not* entitled to 'judge a new response to be "correct" simply because it is the response he is inclined to give' (and others agree). It is correct if it accords with the rule. But we can only speak of accord with a rule in the context of a regular use of a rule as a measure of correctness.

(iii) It has become fashionable in the last decade, under the influence of Michael Dummett, to view Wittgenstein's

---

[63] Ibid., p. 392.
[64] Ibid.

development from the *Tractatus* to the *Philosophical Investigations* as a transformation of a realist into an anti-realist, a truth-conditional theory into an assertability-conditions theory. This has been an unfortunate influence, forcing Wittgenstein into a Procrustean bed, rather than looking carefully to see what he says. Kripke, like others,[65] falls victim to this distorted way of looking at Wittgenstein. Distortions occur at two levels: (a) the representation of the truth-conditional theory in the *Tractatus*; (b) the picture of Wittgenstein's later views on meaning. We shall limit ourselves to some schematic observations.[66]

Kripke characterizes the *Tractatus* with the following thumb-nail sketch:

> The simplest, most basic idea of the *Tractatus* can hardly be dismissed: a declarative sentence gets its meaning by virtue of its *truth conditions*, by virtue of its correspondence to facts that must obtain if it is true. For example, "the cat is on the mat" is understood by those speakers who realize that it is true if and only if a certain cat is on a certain mat; it is false otherwise. The presence of the cat on the mat is a fact or condition-in-the-world that would make the sentence true (express a truth) if it obtained.[67]

Even allowing for the vagaries of sketches, this conflates three distinct doctrines of the *Tractatus*. First, there is the picture theory of the atomic proposition. The sense of such a proposi-

---

[65] Ourselves (in the past) included. Kripke's position differs substantially from Dummett's in respect of the issue of anti-realism, for nothing in his remarks about assertion-conditions commits him to Dummett's anti-realist doctrines. While Dummett's interests lie, as it were, in the geometry of proof, Kripke's lie in the sociology of meaning.

[66] For a detailed analysis of the different *concepts* of truth-conditions, from the *Tractatus*, through Tarski, Carnap and onwards, see G. P. Baker and P. M. S. Hacker, *Language, Sense and Nonsense* (Blackwell, Oxford, 1984), ch. 3).

[67] Kripke, *Wittgenstein*, p. 72.

tion is a function of the meanings of its constituent unanalys-
able names, and it consists in its depiction of an atomic state of
affairs (which may, or may not, obtain). Second, there is a
truth-conditional account of the sense of molecular propositions. Third, there is a correspondence theory of truth. Kripke
treats the *Tractatus* truth-conditional theory as if it were part of
the picture theory of the atomic proposition. But according
to the *Tractatus* it literally makes no sense to talk of the truth-
conditions of an atomic proposition. The truth-conditions of a
proposition are the conditions under which 'T' occurs in the
final column of its truth-table. But there is no such thing as a
truth-table for the atomic proposition 'p'. Similarly Kripke
apparently reads Tarski's T-sentences into the *Tractatus* (viz.
'$F(a)$' is true if and only if $F(a)$). But this is *not* part of the
Tractatus theory of meaning. If T-sentences such as ' "The cat
is on the mat" is true if and only if a certain cat is on a certain
mat' are what spell out truth-conditions, then the truth-
conditional theory parts company with the picture theory of
the proposition, the thesis of isomorphism, the bipolarity of
the proposition and the distinctive (ineffable) *Tractatus* form of
the correspondence theory of truth.

Does this matter? Is it not, after all, just so much history? It
does indeed. For by thus misrepresenting history we facilitate
the fit of the distorting spectacles which allow us to delude
ourselves into viewing the evolution of twentieth century
philosophy of language (philosophical logic) as a progressive
confrontation between truth-conditional semantics and
assertion-conditions semantics.

Kripke contends that the later Wittgenstein 'proposes a
picture of language based, not on *truth conditions*, but on *assertability conditions* or *justification conditions*'.[68] It is very doubtful
whether this picture of Wittgenstein's later views on language
does anything but distort the reality it is meant to represent. It
is true that for some kinds of sentences, in particular third-
person sentences concerning psychological characteristics and

---

[68] Ibid., p. 74.

sentences concerning abilities, we explain their meaning in part by specifying the kinds of circumstance which justify their assertion. But it would be absurd, as well as groundless, to foist on Wittgenstein the view that the meaning of every sentence is given thus. Kripke, to be sure, acknowledges that non-declaratives do not fit into this picture, and avowals of sensation do not either. But the 'exceptions' are not just these. It is not merely avowals of aches and pains that do not fit this mould, but saying that I intend to do so-and-so, remember this or that, want such-and-such. It is not merely psychological predications in the first person that mar the alleged pattern, but hosts of ordinary utterances, such as 'The rose is red', 'The table is round', 'It is warm today', 'My name is N.N.', 'It is time to go' – in short, most sentences. Wittgenstein does *not* claim, with respect to sentences in general, that we explain their meaning by giving their assertion-conditions. The injunction to *look* at how sentences are used is not an implicit claim that all sentences have assertion-conditions. What explanations would we give that would *justify* asserting such sentences as those cited, and *also constitute explanations of their meaning*? (But there is no difficulty in explaining what 'My name is N.N.' or 'It is time to go' or 'The rose is red' mean!)

Forcing Wittgenstein into the invented position of constructivism, intuitionist semantics, assertion-conditions theories, is altogether misguided. It is a mistake stemming from a hankering after sweeping generalizations, global confrontations of semantic theories, and large-scale theory-building. But Wittgenstein builds no such theories. He does not contend that a language is a monolithic structure run through with truth-conditions *or* assertion-conditions which give meanings to sentences and words. It is not a calculus of rules, either in the form of classical logic or in the form of intuitionist logic. It is a motley of language-games, an endlessly variegated form of human activity, interwoven with our lives at every level.

9   A concluding sketch

We have tried to show that Wittgenstein's argument as it struck Kripke is very far removed from Wittgenstein's argument. We have denied that Wittgenstein is concerned with a sceptical problem, and denied that he gives a Humean solution to the problems he was concerned with. To give a proper account of Wittgenstein's discussion of rule-following and its relation to the private language argument would be a large task, which we shall confront in another forum.[69] But perhaps the following sketch may be helpful to a reader who, weary of the flow of denials, yearns for some positive suggestions about Wittgenstein's discussion of rule-following prior to §243.

The conception of meaning which Wittgenstein delineated in the *Tractatus* involved a commitment to various metaphysical doctrines. In particular, fully analysed names were conceived as standing for simple entities in reality which were their meanings. These 'objects' were metaphysical simples, the indestructible substance of reality. The combinatorial possibilities of simple names in a language must mirror the metaphysical combinatorial possibilities of objects in reality. Wittgenstein later referred to this conception as the '*Bedeutungskörper*' (meaning-body) picture. When he returned to philosophy in 1929, the first element of his old way of thinking that he jettisoned was precisely the *Bedeutungskörper* picture. What he argued initially was that instead of conceiving of language as a system of (analysable) signs, connected by means of lines of projection with metaphysical simples that provide simple signs with meanings, we should conceive of language simply as a calculus of rules. The meaning of an expression is not a sempiternal simple object,[70] but the rules

---

[69] See G. P. Baker and P. M. S. Hacker, *An Analytical Commentary on Wittgenstein's Philosophical Investigations*, vol. 2 (forthcoming).

[70] The metaphysical object, he now thought, was an illusion. Its role was filled by *samples*, conceived as belonging to the calculus itself.

for its use, the totality of which fix its place in a calculus of meaning-rules.

Under pressure, this picture too gave way. It gave way, not because a language is not rule-governed, nor because speaking is not a normative activity, but because it involved a mystification of rules no less distorting than the original metaphysics of objects that the normative, calculus conception was meant to replace. <u>Rules for the use of expressions are not bits of normative machinery</u>. They are not Platonic entities whirring away · in <u>Fregean third realms</u>, nor are they psychological entities determining in a causal manner how we are constrained to think. Two deep and ramifying confusions must be extirpated.

It is very tempting to conceive of a sign as standing in a projective relation to what it represents. This conception may be variously realized. Frege conceived the *senses* associated with words as determining references. The *Tractatus* conceived of the proposition as a logical picture representing a state of affairs. The representing picture, the proposition, was held to include the pictorial relationship, 'the correlations of the picture's elements with things' (*Tractatus* 2.1514). *In a like manner*, if one conceives of the meaning of an expression as constituted by the rules for its use, one may think that *the rule* must, in some sense, contain a 'picture' or 'representation' of what complies with it. For understanding an expression must constitute knowing, grasping, the rules that constitute its meaning. Those rules stipulate how the expression is to be used. So by grasping the rules one must grasp how to use, how to apply the expression. But that would only be possible if the rule determines what accords with it, if it fixes what follows from it. Otherwise how could I, by grasping the rule, know what to do with the expression the meaning of which is given by the rule? (Precisely analogous is the thought that an intention, expectation, or order must contain a 'picture' of its fulfilment.)

One of Wittgenstein's central concerns is to probe this conception. We must sharply distinguish the lines of projection from the technique or method of projection. The method of projection is not part of the symbol. Of course, one can describe the method of projection (the application of a symbol). But such a description is itself just another symbol (an interpretation). If the method of application is a bridge between a symbol and what it symbolizes, it is at any rate not built until the application is made. It is not the interpretation that builds the bridge between the sign and what is signified or meant, only the practice does that.[71] It is not rules, of their own accord, that 'determine' meanings, it is the way in which we, in our activities, use rules, that does so. It is not rules that breathe life into signs, but our using the signs in accord with rules, in what we *call* 'accord'. And that is not fixed (magically) by the rule all on its own, by its containing a picture of what accords with it and what does not. It is fixed by our practices of using the rule (the explanation of meaning) to constitute a norm of correctness, our practices of teaching and explaining, of criticizing and correcting, or justifying our applications of an expression by reference to the rule.

A second great confusion is closely connected with the first. We are inclined to think that it is the mind that infuses symbols with their meaning. And when we become anxious that there is a gap between an explanation of the meaning of an expression and the use of the expression, it is altogether natural to think that it is the mind that bridges that gap, that effects the connection between a rule and its application. This can be variously conceived. Frege thought of a sense as an abstract entity which determines a referent, or presents a referent in a certain way. Grasping a sense he thought of as an altogether mysterious[72] mental act of coming into contact with such entities. Indeed, it would not be unlikely imagining a sign *together with its lines of projection* (compare *Investigations* §141) save that a sense, being

[71] Wittgenstein, MS 165, p. 82.

[72] Frege, *Posthumous Writings*, ed. H. Hermes et al. (Blackwell, Oxford, 1979), p. 145.

an abstract object, is not imaginable. In the *Tractatus* meaning is conferred on signs by the will, the 'metaphysical self' that thinks the method of projection in thinking of the sense of the proposition (*Tractatus* 3.11). The wayward antagonist in *Investigations* §§184–243 conceives of the mind as 'drawing the projection lines' from the symbol, or from the rule which explains its use, to its application. This is held to be done by mental acts or processes of understanding, by acts of meaning (e.g. addition by 'plus') or by intuitive insight.

Pricking the bubble of these philosophical flights of fancy is one of the tasks Wittgenstein undertakes in the *Investigations* discussion of rule-following. One by one he examines these false pictures of understanding and of rules, and shows that they constitute a mythology of symbolism. He does not deny that we can and often do 'grasp the whole use of a word in a flash', or that when we order someone to expand the series '+2' we mean him to go on '20004, 20006'. We can and do explain how a given rule is to be followed, and we can and do learn how to follow rules correctly (independently of intuitions and causal necessitations). But these mundane phenomena must be seen aright, not from the perspective of the mysteries of rules, nor yet of the mysteries of understanding. It is *acting* according to a rule, a *practice* of normative behaviour, that lies at the bottom of our language-games. Language, far from being a reflection of thought, is a form of behaviour. It is no coincidence that Wittgenstein often quoted the line from Goethe: *Im Anfang war die Tat*.

Kripke contends that Wittgenstein has invented a new form of scepticism ('the most radical and original sceptical problem that philosophy has seen to date'), that 'it is important to see that his achievement in posing this problem stands on its own, independently of the value of his own solution of it and the resultant argument against private language'.[73] This observation not only misrepresents the character of Wittgenstein's preoccupations and achievements, but also fails to appreciate

[73] Kripke, *Wittgenstein*, p. 60.

the diminishing significance of scepticism in philosophy. Philosophical scepticism played a significant role in seventeenth century culture, stimulated in part by the deep need for a criterion of truth within religion (given the schism within Christianity), for a criterion of truth for scientific theories (given the number of competing scientific theories, e.g. of the solar system, all equally reliable within acceptable margins of error), and for a criterion of truth between science and religion. But perhaps the most important impetus was the manifest conflict between the new scientific picture of reality (as consisting of material objects possessing only geometric and mechanical properties, and powers to affect our sensibility in such-and-such colourful ways) and our ordinary conception of the world. No one could gainsay the colossal achievements of the new science, but it seemed to open a gulf between appearance and reality which required explanation and justification. For if the world as it is in itself is so different from the world as it appears to be, how can we be certain that we can ever know anything about it as it really is? In this cultural context it was altogether natural that philosophy should become preoccupied with justifying the ways of God (and His world) in the face of sceptical doubts.

Those days are long past. Scepticism, in the twentieth century, is no longer a *serious* issue in our culture (save perhaps in the domains of ethics and aesthetics). One may *use* scepticism as a colourful device to present a genuine problem. But this manoeuvre is no more than heuristic. Achievement in philosophy today *could not* consist in inventing new forms of scepticism. The deepest cultural preoccupations of this century turn on issues concerning language and communication. These ramify through literature and art (from von Hoffmannsthal and Joyce to Orwell, Borges, Beckett or Pinter as well as such artists as Picasso, de Chirico and Magritte, Steinberg and Escher), through the 'humane studies', psychology, linguistics and sociology. It is not surprising that philosophy has followed suit, not like the owl of Minerva, but in fruitful symbiotic relationship with the rest of our culture. Wittgenstein's *central* concerns,[74] in both his philosophies, were with the nature of language, its function and structure (cf. *Investigations* §92), and the myriad philosophical illusions propensity to which is the unavoidable condition of every language-user. It is here, and not in the *invention* of new forms of scepticism, that his achievements lie. His reflections on rule-following not only undermine a conception of language rampant in philosophy, theoretical linguistics, and psychology, but also yield a novel and more profound conception of logical and mathematical necessity than any yet achieved by philosophers. His private language argument, the *real* private language argument, not only undermines a tradition of philosophical thought running from Descartes to the present day, but yields novel and more profound conceptions of self-consciousness, of the relation of mind to body, and of the will than any available hitherto. What exactly his conception was needs exposition, which we have not offered save *en passant*. Whether his conception was right needs argument, which we have not given, save *per accidens*. What we have done is to show that it does not lie in the arid area of sceptical questions, let alone of Humean sceptical solutions.

[74] This is not to say that his discussions of scepticism in *On Certainty* are unimportant, merely that it would be misconceived to represent these themes as lying at the heart of the *Philosophical Investigations*.

2

The Illusions of Rule-scepticism

1 The 'rule-following considerations' reconsidered

The concept of a rule informs our reflections on most distinctively human, significant, phenomena. We are, above all, rule-making and rule-following creatures. A language is a multi-levelled rule-governed practice of using symbols. So too are formal calculi. Morality, social life, law, games are run through with rules and related normative phenomena. If, in reflecting on these features of our lives, our concepts of a rule and of what it is to follow a rule are awry, so will much else be too. An incorrect logical point of view upon rules will guarantee an incorrect conception of ourselves, our minds and our normative practices. It will also ensure deep misunderstanding of the nature of speech, inference and calculation. Furthermore, clarification of the nature of normative phenomena, in particular of the nature of *explanations* of rule-governed practices, is the pivotal issue in the venerable controversy between methodological monists and methodological pluralists in the matter of the relationship between the moral sciences (*Geisteswissenschaften*) and the natural sciences (*Naturwissenschaften*). In short, the concept of a rule is of central and fundamental importance.

It follows immediately both that the philosophical clarification of the concept of a rule is a suitable Large Topic to engage philosophers (that 'Rules' is an appropriate chapter title for a philosophical grammar) and that any radically new insight into rules will have substantial repercussions on a wide range of philosophical reflections. Wittgenstein's extensive discussions of rules is now perceived to be the focus of such a conceptual earthquake, and hence there has recently been a flood tide of interest in his 'rule-following considerations'. Among many philosophers[1] the conviction has spread that he is propounding a novel form of scepticism about rule-following. This scepticism, they claim, is not dissolved or shown to be nonsense, but rather is accepted and by-passed by Wittgenstein. Rule-scepticism is thought to have force only against an atomistic or individualistic conception of rule-following. Wittgenstein's alleged 'sceptical solution' to his newly discovered scepticism consists in the argument that the existence of a community of rule-followers is bound up with the very concept of following a rule, i.e. that it makes sense to speak of someone's following a rule only if his actions are related to the behaviour of a community of rule-followers. Rule-scepticism and 'the community view' are thought to be the foci of Wittgenstein's philosophical investigations, and the interest of these topics has put hitherto neglected remarks in his writings into the philosophical limelight.

The initial, most fundamental, philosophical question which has shaped current discussions is typically put thus: What is it for a rule to determine an act as being in accord with it? Or again: What is *accord with a rule*, and what fixes it? How can a formulation of a rule, the 'mere words' with which we express a rule, determine of indefinitely many acts that they accord with or contravene a rule? Here, as in the case of other

[1] For example, Robert Fogelin, *Wittgenstein* (Routledge and Kegan Paul, London, 1976), ch. XII; Crispin Wright, *Wittgenstein on the Foundations of Mathematics* (Duckworth, London, 1980), chs II, XII; Saul A. Kripke, *Wittgenstein on Rules and Private Language* (Blackwell, Oxford, 1982); and Christopher Peacocke, 'Rule-Following: The Nature of Wittgenstein's Arguments', in *Wittgenstein: to Follow a Rule*, ed. S. H. Holtzman and C. M. Leich (Routledge and Kegan Paul, London, 1981); H. Putnam, 'Convention: a theme in philosophy' in *Realism and Reason* (Cambridge University Press, Cambridge, 1983).

aspects of the 'harmony between language and reality',[2] we must apparently find a safe passage between the Scylla of Platonism and the Charybdis of mentalism.

Platonism may lure us to perdition through the suggestion that it is not, of course, the rule-formulation that determines what is to count as accord with the rule, but rather the rule itself, which is *expressed* by the rule-formulation. A rule, it is held, is an abstract entity, and *it* determines of its own accord, what follows from it. Thus, for example, Frege, the arch-Platonist of modern philosophy of mathematics, viewed his axiomatization of the propositional calculus as an endeavour to arrive at

> a small number of laws in which . . . the content of all the laws is included, albeit in an undeveloped state . . . Since in view of the boundless multitude of laws that can be enunciated we cannot list them all, we cannot achieve completeness except by searching out those that, *by their power*, contain all of them.[3]

On this view the axioms of the calculus constitute a powerful logical machine, the atemporal workings of which generate the theorems of logic.

Mentalism may lure us into confusion through the suggestion that it is not, of course, the rule-formulation (the mere words!), but rather what we mean by these words, that determines what is to count as accord with the rule. When I order someone to follow a certain rule (which I specify in words), I *mean* him to do particular things in various circumstances, and

[2] For example, the 'harmony', the match, between a proposition and the fact that makes it true, or between an order and the act which complies with it, or between an expectation and the event which fulfils it, or between a desire and what satisfies it. The general topic is examined in detail in Essay 3 below.

[3] G. Frege, *Begriffsschrift, eine der arithmetischen nachgebildete Formelsprache des reinen Denkens*, §13, in G. Frege, *Conceptual Notation and Related Articles*, tr. T. W. Bynum (Clarendon Press, Oxford, 1972).

it is this that fixes what is to count as accord. When I tell someone to expand the arithmetical series of the even integers, I *mean* him to write '1002' after '1000', '20468' after '20466', and so on. The mind, on this view, is a mysterious and wonderful instrument (perhaps even a biological computer) that can perform an infinite number of acts of meaning in an instant. Are there any safe waters between the rocks of logical machinery and the whirlpools of the magic of the mind?

This (as yet opaque) array of questions may seem excessively narrow to carry within it the seeds of such ramifying consequences. A step or two more may indicate the trajectory of the chain of problems. If at first blush the odd questions of what it is for an act to be in accord with a rule, and of what it is for something to be a consequence of a rule, seem insufficiently momentous, reflection should persuade one otherwise. For inasmuch as mastery of a language is mastery of a rule-governed technique, then a clear understanding of what it is for an act to be determined as being in accord with a rule must be a prerequisite for a proper grasp of the very notion of understanding. Moreover, since the notions of validity and logical consequence are fundamental to our conceptions of thinking, reasoning and inferring, and since they are themselves normative notions, a clear understanding of what it is for an inference pattern to be valid is fundamental for a proper grasp of our cognitive capacities. And since our notion of logical and mathematical necessity is bound up with our notion of rule-governed consequence, clarification of what it is for something to be necessitated by a rule must hold the key to understanding the nature of necessity.

We do not intend pursuing all these great questions here.[4] Our aim is the more modest one of examining the premises of the current discussion of rule-scepticism, the sceptical conclusions typically derived from them, and the alleged sceptical resolu-

---

[4] They are, however, discussed in our forthcoming *Analytical Commentary on Wittgenstein's Philosophical Investigations*, vol. 2 (Blackwell, Oxford).

tion of these worries by means of versions of the 'community view' of rule-following. Our objective is to demonstrate that the mainstream contemporary debate is flowing down the wrong channels into marshlands and bogs, achieving little but the muddying of the waters. Not only are Wittgenstein's arguments and conclusions totally distorted, but the 'community view', 'the sceptical solution', and 'the rule-following considerations' held up as *his* views are ones which he explicitly repudiated. Indeed, they are multiply incoherent for reasons which he articulated. Our concern here is to show that the arguments deployed in defence of these views manifest deep misunderstandings of normative concepts and of normative phenomena.

2   Rule-scepticism set up

The source of current rule-scepticism lies in a battery of puzzles concerning the relationship between a rule and its applications (its 'extension' as Wittgenstein sometimes calls it). One might be tempted to state the fundamental question in this form: How can a rule contain a picture of what accords with it? This question seems to lead straight into a dilemma. On the one hand, it seems as if a rule must contain a picture of what accords with it (just as it seems that a proposition must contain a picture of the state of affairs that makes it true). For, if one understands a rule, one knows what accords with it and what contravenes it (putting aside borderline cases). On the other hand, this seems impossible. For it seems that one is given only the bare *formulation*, something that both needs to be interpreted and can be interpreted in indefinitely many different ways! *Any* action can be brought into accord with any rule by means of some interpretation or other.[5] There is, for example, nothing sacrosanct about reading a key of interpretation thus

[5] See Wittgenstein, *Philosophical Investigations*, tr. G. E. M. Anscombe (Blackwell, Oxford, 1958), §198.

⇛ rather than thus ⇄ .[6] If I point at a pencil and say 'This is tove', how does this rule for the use of the word 'tove' (i.e. this ostensive definition) determine whether 'tove' is to be used to denote the colour of the pencil, its shape, length, the stuff of which it is made, etc.?[7] And if I explain to a pupil the rule of the series of even integers, what determines that the right way to continue after '1000' is '1002, 1004, . . .' rather than '1004, 1008, . . .'? One can, it seems, bring '1004, 1008 . . .' into accord with the order 'Add 2!' (with the specification of the rule of the series + 2). For one can interpret the rule-formulation to mean: add 2 up to 1000, and thereafter add 4. But if this, in general, is so, how can a rule guide one? How can it show one what to do? How can one know whether a certain act is correct according to a rule? A picture which can be made out to represent *anything*, represents nothing. So should we conclude, absurdly, that rules cannot guide us; or that they do not determine such-and-such acts as being in accord? Wittgenstein dismisses this argument as a *misunderstanding*. It is wrong to suppose that a rule and its extension are essentially connected only through the mediation of an interpretation.[8] But of Wittgenstein's reject, others have made the keystone of their arch.

What Wittgenstein is supposed to reject is the assumption that an act accords with a rule if there is *some* interpretation of the rule with which it squares. The appealing solution is to rid the fallacious account of the indeterminacy of existential generalization by pinning down *one* authoritative interpretation. The crucial question then seems to be: *whose* interpretation. But this strategy leaves undisturbed the dubious premise that an interpretation is necessary in order to relate a rule to an action. And it is primarily the apparent indeterminacy of

[6] *Ibid.*, §86.
[7] Cf. Wittgenstein, *The Blue and Brown Books* (Blackwell, Oxford, 1958), p. 2.
[8] Cf. Wittgenstein, *Philosophical Investigations*, §§198, 201.

anybody's interpretation (both first- and third-person cases) which leads, by slightly different routes, to rule-scepticism.

(i) Suppose that someone is writing out what appears to be (and is) a part of the series of even integers. When he reaches 1000, he continues '1004, 1008, . . .'. Is this correct? Or suppose that someone is apparently adding, but only numbers the sum of which is less than 110. Now, for the first time he encounters '56 + 56'. What is the correct thing to write? We might propose that the answer should depend solely on whether his answer accords with *his* understanding of the rule, i.e. that the agent's own interpretation of the rule provides the criterion of what is correct. But then, of course, we must determine precisely how he does interpret the rule (since it is always open to various interpretations), i.e. *which* rule he is following. All the evidence we have to go on as to his interpretation of the rule (the rule of the series, given by the formulation ' +2' or by a series of examples '2, 4, 6, 8, 10, and so on'; or the rule for the arithmetical operation of addition given by examples, or by an algorithm) is the applications made of it hitherto. That the sign ' +', for example, expresses the addition function, that the rule for the use of ' +' correlates this sign with that function, is an hypothesis, resting on the data of his past applications of ' +'. But like all scientific hypotheses, it is underdetermined by the data. For given that this person has never calculated with numbers the sum of which is greater than 110, how can we say whether he takes '56 + 56' to yield '112' or, say, '5'? So how, in general, can one be sure *which* rule another person is following? On this view, it should be noted, there is no doubt that the addition function maps pairs of numbers uniquely on to a number (quite independently of us), or that the series of even integers continues '1002, 1004, . . .'. The problem is, how can we be sure that by ' +' he *means* the addition function, or by writing '. . . 776, 778, 780 . . .' he means to be applying the rule ' +2'.

(ii) The first route to rule-scepticism may seem to involve a curious marriage of Platonism about functions and rules with empiricism about evidence. Feeling distaste for

Platonic realms of functions determining values for pairs of arguments independently of us, we might simply drop the Platonism. We might accept that in the past one's use of '+', what is called 'addition', was rule-governed, determining such-and-such answers (the precedents) as correct. The past applications of '+' are evidence for what one meant by '+'. But how can one determine, on the basis of what one *meant*, how one is to apply the expression to a new case? Different interpretations are consistent with the past applications of '+', and what one meant by '+' is, it seems, indeterminate between such different interpretations. So how can one's interpretations of the rule for what is called 'addition' tell one what it is correct to do in a fresh case? How can an interpretation fixed only by a limited set of precedents reach forward to indefinitely many new cases, determining in advance what the agent will count as correct applications of the rules?

These two routes to rule-scepticism, when considered with respect to other people, produce a radical scepticism about determining whether others really understand rule-governed signs at all, whether they understand them as one does oneself, what they understand by such-and-such signs, and how they interpret the rules they seem to be following. Observing N.N.'s past activities of calculations with numbers smaller than 55, how can we determine whether by '+' he means the addition function or some other function? How can we know that by 'blue' he means blue, and not some bizarre Goodmanian 'colour' such as 'bleen' (i.e. blue until today, and green henceforth)? For the data of past performances do not give adequate inductive support for the hypothesis that this rule, *thus interpreted*, is being followed.

(iii) We are prone to think that this predicament arises only with respect to others. It seems a version of puzzles about other minds transferred, as it were, to what others mean by the symbols they use, what rules they intend to follow, and what interpretations they impose. But surely, one is inclined to think, in *my own case*, I know which rule I am following and what act is in accord with it! But has not Quine taught us that radical translation begins at home? And has not Wittgenstein taught us that first-person privileges are constitutionally *ultra vires*? I myself, in respect of my own normative behaviour, am in fact no better off than I am in respect of others. What do *I* mean by the signs I use? I can give myself the rule-formulation, but that can be differently interpreted. So what is my interpretation? I can, of course, use the sign, e.g. '+' or 'red', as I have used it in the past, relying on precedents set by my past performances. But in this respect I am in exactly the same position as the agent considered in (i) and (ii) above.

(iv) The supposition that rule-scepticism only applies to other people's normative behaviour comes under fire from another direction. Each of us is inclined (correctly) to think that he knows what he means by what he says. But, it is argued, the nub of Wittgenstein's private language argument, stated briefly in the *Philosophical Investigations* §202, is that *this possibility* obtains only in the context of a social practice:

> And hence also 'obeying a rule' is a practice. And to *think* one is obeying a rule is not to obey a rule. Hence it is not possible to obey the rule 'privately': otherwise thinking one was obeying a rule would be the same thing as obeying it.[9]

Only against the background of a community practice is it possible genuinely to mean something by a sign, to follow a rule. As far as a solitary individual is concerned, considered independently of a rule-following, language-using community, *there is no distinction* between following a rule and seeming to follow a rule, between being correct and seeming to be correct. So introspection cannot fix a determinate inter-

[9] That interpreting this passage to be concerned with *social* practices, and taking 'following a rule "privately"' to mean 'independently of a community practice' is a gross distortion of its meaning is argued above, pp. 20f. For a detailed analysis of this passage and the argument of which it is a part, see Baker and Hacker, *Analytical Commentary on Wittgenstein's Philosophical Investigations*, vol. 2 (forthcoming).

pretation of the rule that I set myself to follow (since it *ipso facto* involves considering myself in isolation from any community). Whatever I think to be in accord with my interpretation will be in accord with it, and that means that there is no sense to the distinction between correct and incorrect, if drawn by reference to accord with my interpretation. It is a corollary of this point that there can be no such thing as a solitary individual's following a rule at all.

3   The alleged solution to the sceptical predicament

The various lines of argument apparently converge on the same conclusion, lending each other mutual support. A mere formulation of a rule cannot determine what is in accord with the rule, since it can be variously interpreted. But what determines the correct interpretation? No individual's past intentions, his meaning such-and-such, can alone constitute a determinate, definitive, interpretation of a rule which will determine correctness and incorrectness. Similarly, although precedents in a person's past applications of a rule allegedly settle the correctness or incorrectness of repeated applications, they cannot determine the correctness of novel applications. So, as long as correctness can be judged only relative to somebody's interpretation of a rule, there will always be cases in anybody's behaviour where there is no distinction between his seeming to follow the rule (on some fixed interpretation) and his actually following the rule. In particular, any agent's own reflections on his apparent, intended, rule-following behaviour must leave him in this predicament. Considered in isolation, he cannot be said to act in accord with or contrary to a rule, since his seeming to follow a rule is both objectively and subjectively indistinguishable from his actually following it. These conclusions are a new form of scepticism. Whether Wittgenstein invented it is an interesting exegetical and historical question of no essential philosophical moment. The fact is that they pose an urgent problem for philosophical reflection. Or so it seems!

For those who conceive these 'rule-following considerations' to be cogent, the crucial requirement to salvage the concept of acting in accord with a rule is thought to be fixing on something which plays the role of an interpretation, but which is *nobody's* interpretation. This requirement is allegedly satisfied by taking into consideration the full range of precedents evident in the behaviour of an entire community in applying the rule whose 'interpretation' is sought. The *standard* behaviour in response to particular circumstances supplies an impersonal or supra–personal yardstick against which each individual's responses can be adjudged correct or incorrect. By considering each rule-follower as a member of a community of rule-followers, we can resuscitate the half-drowned concept of correctness from the tides of scepticism, and maintain a sharp boundary between someone's thinking that he conforms with a rule and his actually conforming with it.

There is a chorus of assent to the 'community view'. Wright contends that:

> There cannot be such a thing as a first-person privileged recognition of the dictates of one's understanding of an expression; irrespective of whether that understanding is shared . . .
> . . . None of us can make sense of the idea of correct employment of language save by reference to the authority of securable community assent on the matter.[10]

This conception is echoed by Peacocke:

> What it is for a person to be following a rule, even individually, cannot ultimately be explained without reference to some community.
> . . . only by appealing to the fact that the genuine rule-follower agrees in his reactions to examples with

[10] Wright, *Wittgenstein on the Foundations of Mathematics*, pp. 217, 220.

the members of some community can we say what distinguishes him from someone who falsely thinks he is following a rule.[11]

And Kripke too concurs:

> the answer is that, if one person is considered in isolation, the notion of a rule as guiding the person who adopts it can have *no* substantive content . . .
>
> The situation is very different if we widen our gaze from consideration of the rule follower alone and allow ourselves to consider him as interacting with a wider community. Others will then have justification conditions for attributing correct or incorrect rule following to the subject . . .
>
> . . . Any individual who claims to have mastered the concept of . . . will be judged by the community to have done so if his particular responses agree with those of the community in enough cases . . .[12]

This chorus of assent, however, must not be allowed to mask differences of key.

One dimension of difference relates to a distinction between actuality and potentiality. On the one hand, only actual precedents in the behaviour of members of the community might be held relevant to settling the standard response which is definitive of correctness of applications of a rule. This might be called 'normative actualism'. (It would have the consequence that the distinction between correct and incorrect would peter out where precedents are lacking.) On the other hand, correctness might be explained by reference to standing dispositions of members of the community to make particular applications of rules, even in previously unencountered circumstances. This might be called 'the community disposition thesis'.

[11] Peacocke, 'Rule-Following', p. 73; cf. Fogelin, *Wittgenstein*, p. 144.
[12] Kripke, *Wittgenstein*, pp. 89, 91f.

On this view, 'to follow a given rule' means 'to act in a way in which members of one's linguistic community are disposed to act in response to such-and-such operative facts'. The meaning of an expression, Peacocke contends, 'is not determined just by the examples given in explanation of the word in question, but by those examples *together with* the disposition of members of the community to go on in certain ways and not others'.[13]

Accordingly, the distinction between following a rule and thinking one is following a rule is the distinction between responding to certain operative facts as other rule-followers are disposed to respond and responding differently. Hence the expression 'red', e.g., means: what most people call 'red' (normative actualism) or are disposed to call 'red' (the community disposition thesis). Democratic principles, *mirabile dictu*, are enshrined in logic!

A further variant of the community view distances itself from the community disposition thesis by repudiating the claim that community consensus enters into the truth-conditions of judgments that particular acts are in accord with particular rules. Kripke's version of the community view denies that judgments of this kind have any truth-conditions at all. Instead, agreement enters into an explanation of the 'assertability conditions' of such sentences as 'This act conforms with this rule':

> each of us *automatically* calculates new addition problems (without feeling the need to check with the community whether our procedure is proper); . . . the community feels entitled to correct a deviant calculation; . . . in practice such deviation is rare, and so on. Wittgenstein thinks that these observations about sufficient conditions for justified assertion are enough to illuminate the role and utility in our lives of assertion about meaning and determination of new answers. What follows from these

[13] Peacocke, 'Rule Following', p. 92.

assertability conditions is *not* that the answer everyone gives to an addition problem is, by definition, the correct one, but rather the platitude that, if everyone agrees upon a certain answer, then no one will feel justified in calling the answer wrong.[14]

On this account, there is, in effect, *no* explanation of what it is to apply a rule correctly. That would require pinning down a single interpretation of the rule over the entire (infinite) range of its application, and this, it is argued, is impossible. All that can be said is that if one applies the rule as others are disposed to apply it, no one will be *justified* in objecting. (It is noteworthy that the denial of a truth-conditional account, understood as a denial that there are any necessary and sufficient conditions for the truth of 'A applied rule R correctly' is perfectly general. So, presumably, there are no truth-conditions for correctly applying the rule of addition even to familiar old cases, e.g. '10 + 15'; a surprising conclusion since it seems uncontroversial enough to suppose that what is both necessary and sufficient here is answering '25'!)

Four general features are worth noting. First, although an individual may apply a rule correctly or incorrectly (or, no one may be justified in asserting that he has misapplied the rule), there is no such thing as the community in general applying a rule incorrectly. Community behaviour is the court of last appeal, and hence it cannot be judged to be correct or incorrect. Wright draws this conclusion explicitly: 'we . . . reject the idea that, in the senses requisite for investigation-independence, the community goes right or wrong in accepting a particular verdict on a decidable question; rather, it just goes'.[15]

Secondly, and complementary to the first feature, the only thing that stands between the terminus of justification of a normative practice and irrationality is social solidarity. Scepti-

[14] Kripke, *Wittgenstein*, pp. 111f.
[15] Wright, *Wittgenstein on the Foundations of Mathematics*, p. 220.

cal doubts about the justification of our normative procedures can always be raised. Our justifications inevitably terminate in patterns of reasoning sanctioned by community behaviour (or the dispositions inferred therefrom). But these too can be challenged by a tough-minded sceptic. And at this point we can give him no further justification. All we can do is huddle together and announce in unison: 'This is what *we* do'.[16]

Thirdly, there is a noteworthy similarity between these variants of 'the community view' of rules and familiar *fallacious* solutions to analogous problems which Wittgenstein subsumed under the heading of 'the harmony between language and reality', and which he condemned root and branch. The questions are such as: 'How can a proposition determine (contain a picture of) what will make it true?', 'How can we think of what is not the case?', or 'How can an expectation anticipate what will satisfy it?'. The typical suggestions to resolve these strange questions consist in postulating intermediate entities. Thus it might seem that what must mediate between the proposition and what makes it true is a *possible state of affairs* which it depicts. It may appear that what we think, when we think of what is not the case, is a *proposition, the sense of a sentence*, for it will exist even if what we think to be the case is not the case. And what mediates between desire and its fulfilment is a feeling of satisfaction.[17] So too, in the case of a rule, what mediates between a rule and its 'extension' is community assent. Or, put slightly differently, this resolution of the rule-sceptical conundrums accepts the view Wittgenstein explicitly rejects, namely that a rule can be applied only in so far as its application is mediated by an interpretation. And community assent fulfils the role of an 'objective' interpretation (what we called 'nobody's interpretation'). Finally, normative actualism provides no standard of correctness for applying any rule the

---

[16] A conception reminiscent of A. J. Ayer's 'Descriptive Analysis' strategy against scepticism, cf. his *The Problem of Knowledge*, (Penguin, Harmondsworth, 1957), pp. 80f.

[17] See below, pp. 108f.

range of applications of which is unlimited. It merely enlarges the pool of precedents. The community disposition thesis hardly fares better. For it is doubtful whether one can give an adequate account of what *is* correct by reference to what people *would* do in certain circumstances, unless it is pre-supposed that their disposition is to comply with an independently fixed standard of correctness. Moreover, independently of a given rule it is unclear how to determine in advance what the community disposition is in respect of hitherto unen-countered cases. Although both views aim to establish an objective standard of correctness in the face of sceptical doubts, the form of objectivity looks distinctly flaccid.

The contention of this essay is that on every issue this account, in all its variant forms, is an interwoven, ramifying series of gross misunderstandings of normativity. The ultimate irony is that it is precisely these kinds of misunderstandings that Wittgenstein laboured to expose in the *Philosophical Investigations*.

4   Flaws in the 'community view'

Having set up the Sceptic Triumphant, the 'sceptical solution' to the problem consists in invoking social services. In the face of scepticism about rule-following, it is held, safety lies in numbers. Closer scrutiny of this strategy, however, reveals glaring flaws. The putative solution to the sceptical problem is patently misguided.

First, it is false that 'to follow a rule correctly' means 'to do as most people do or are disposed to do when they endeavour to follow it'. The community disposition thesis wrongly as-similates the *normative* notion of following a rule correctly with the statistical notion of acting in the same way as most people are disposed to do in such-and-such conditions. The statistical conception makes the statement that acting thus-and-so is in accord with such-and-such a rule into an empirical statement. Not only is it not empirical (being, instead, a 'grammatical' truth), but also it is not statistical. Most people who carry out such a computation as 0.07642 ⌐158.647521 are probably schoolchildren, and very likely most of them make mistakes. They are duly corrected by their teachers, of course. But it is no use adjusting the community disposition thesis to read: correct following of a rule consists in acting as most *competent* followers of that rule act. For a competent follower of a certain rule is one who standardly follows it *correctly*, i.e. we determine skill or competence here by reference to the antecedent notion of correctness.

Secondly, it is false that we have no notion of correctness at all, but only a notion of assertion-conditions for correctness and incorrectness, i.e. that if one acts as everyone else does or is inclined to do, no one will be justified in challenging one, and conversely, if one acts contrary to the statistical norm, there will be a justification for calling that answer wrong. But the concept of a rule and the concept of what accords with it (what is a correct application of it) are internally related. Understanding a rule and knowing what accords with it are, in this respect, akin to intending and knowing what will fulfil one's intention, or expecting something and knowing what will satisfy one's expectation. There is no such thing as expecting it to rain tomorrow, but not knowing that its raining tomorrow will satisfy one's expectation. It is inconceivable that I should intend to take an umbrella with me when I go for a walk, yet not know that my intention will be fulfilled or executed only by my taking an umbrella with me; and so on. So too, there is no such thing as understanding a rule correctly, but being in general at a loss over how to apply it (hard cases need not concern us here). An ostensive definition of the word 'red' by reference to a paradigmatic sample is a rule for the use of this word. But it is not possible that someone should understand this explanation (rule) correctly yet not know what counts as correct applications of 'red'. A pupil who calls blue objects 'red' will be judged not to have understood the ostensive definition. It is not true that 'red' means 'what most people call "red" ', nor is it true that we cannot say what it is for this rule to be correctly applied. For 'red' is correctly applied to an object (an apple, say) if and only if the object is the colour of the defining sample. Similarly, a correct application of the word 'metre' consists in ascribing to an object the property of being n metres long just in case it is n times the length of the standard metre (or of one's correctly calibrated metre stick).

Thirdly, and consequently, it is true that '. . . meaning is not determined just by the examples given in explanation of the word in question'[18], but it is false that it is determined 'by those examples *together with* the disposition of members of the community to go on in certain ways and not others'. This conception fails even to grasp the point that typically explanations by examples involve using a series of examples *as a formulation of the rule*. The examples, thus viewed, are no more *applications* of the rule explained than is an ostensive definition of 'red' (by pointing at a tomato) an application (predication) of 'red'. Nevertheless, it is in a qualified sense true that meaning is not 'determined' just by a formulation of a rule, not even by a formulation by means of a series of examples. (Of course, one may give the meaning of the problematic expression thus; but whether one grasps the meaning thus given remains to be seen.) The formulation of a rule must itself be *used* in a certain manner, as a canon of correct use. Its status *as* a rule-formulation depends upon its use. Reflect on the fact that explaining what 'one metre' means by pointing at a metre-rod and saying 'That (length) is one metre' is perfectly correct, but both *understanding* this explanation and using this sentence *as an explanation* require grasp of the manner in which measuring rods are *used* to measure the lengths of objects. (Namely, by being laid alongside them, and the length read off the calibrating marks in such-and-such a way.) Rules are used in teaching, in which the pattern of relations between the rule (given by a rule-formulation) and its extension is exhibited, and what counts as *applying the rule* or *doing the same* is manifest. They are used in justifying, correcting, and sometimes even in applica-

---

[18] Peacocke, 'Rule Following', p. 92.

tions. This is not a matter of collective dispositions, but of a normative practice, which may be collective, but need not be. The complement of the insight that the meaning of an expression is its use in accord with a norm is the insight that what is called 'the rule for the use of an expression' must itself be something that is used in a certain manner to monitor the use of an expression.

Fourthly, the claim that the community as a whole cannot be wrong in accepting a particular verdict on a decidable question is confused. If the leader of the community instructed his people to sacrifice to the gods on midsummer's day, they may well miscalculate the day, and later discover that they had misapplied the law (equally, just one of them might make this discovery, and despite his being right, be disbelieved by the rest). So, up to a point, general consensus is compatible with misapplication.

Yet, there is a significant point here, although it is not one which bears out the community view. While the community (most speakers of the language) may occasionally misapply a rule, be wrong in holding such-and-such a verdict to be a correct application, the community cannot in general be mistaken over *what its rules are*. Nor can it, *in general*, be mistaken about what is a correct application of its rules, since rules and applications are internally related.[19] We may discover that the ancient Persians played chess according to somewhat different rules than ours. This does not show that we are playing incorrectly, or that we are not 'really' playing chess; but only that our version of chess differs somewhat from the original game. There is no truth *behind* the rules which makes just these rules 'correct'. We make our rules. They may be interesting or dull, useful or useless, ingenious or foolish, but not true or correct.

---

[19] But then neither can an individual. He may be mistaken about what the common shared rules of a certain game are. But not over what rules he is following, nor over what *he* takes to be acting in accord with them – unless he simply falls into total confusion.

Nevertheless, consensus in application is an important aspect of mutual understanding. Understanding of a rule is exhibited in two complementary ways, in giving and explaining formulations of the rule and in applying the rule in practice. Whether two people understand a given rule in the same way is manifest not only in the fact that they explain or interpret it similarly, but also in the fact that they apply it identically. 'If language is to be a means of communication', Wittgenstein observed, 'there must be agreement not only in definitions but also . . . in judgments'.[20] But he was fully aware of the philosophical pitfalls surrounding this claim, pitfalls which endanger defenders of the 'community view'.

In the first place, 'This seems to abolish logic', presumably by apparently abolishing the *objectivity* of rule-following. But this, Wittgenstein insists, is an illusion. 'To follow a rule' does *not* mean 'to do what most people call "to follow a rule" '. Community agreement yields a sense of objectivity (or assertion-conditions for correctness) only by severing the internal relation between the rule and what accords with it. In place of that internal relation the community view substitutes the notion of community *agreement*, which is not an *internal property* of the rule. Community agreement shows that the members of the community are all playing the same game, as it were, but that they should agree in applying the rules of the game is not itself one of the rules of the game. It is a framework condition within which the community game is possible. But that acting thus-and-so *is* acting in accord with *this* rule is no more a matter of what people are disposed to do than that the fact that *p* is the fact that makes the proposition that *p* true is a matter of what people are disposed to believe.

Secondly, it seems to imply that 'human agreement decides what is true and what is false'. But this, of course, is nonsense. It is the world that determines *truth*; human agreement determines meaning. A correct account of rules and their relation to their extension, a proper *Übersicht* of understanding and

[20] Wittgenstein, *Philosophical Investigations*, §242.

following rules, must do justice to the fact that what we call 'following a rule' presupposes a certain constancy in the results of following a rule,[21] without collapsing truth into consensus, abrogating the *internal* relations between rules and their applications, or detracting from the objectivity of rule-following. This the community view fails to do.

Equally misguided is the suggestion that only against the background of community rule-following can one distinguish following a rule from thinking that one is following a rule. It is claimed that

> the only thing that must be true of someone who is trying to follow a rule, so long as we consider just the individual and not facts about some community, is that he is disposed to think that certain cases fall under the rule and others do not. But this is something which is also true of a person who falsely believes that he is conforming to a rule.[22]

Only conformity with what other members of the community do gives sense to 'following a rule'. In general, 'there cannot be such a thing as a first-person privileged recognition of the dictates of one's understanding of an expression, irrespective of whether that understanding is shared'.[23] What such rule-scepticism fails to see is that even to *try* to follow a rule requires that one have some understanding of the rule one is purporting to follow, some conception of what is to count as acting in accord with it. To understand a rule is to grasp an internal relation between the rule and its (potential) extension. This is something *stipulated*, not discovered, *a fortiori* not a matter of dispositions, either public or private. Whether a person is following a rule, or only thinks incorrectly that he is following a rule, does not depend on what others are or might be doing.

[21] Ibid.
[22] Peacocke, 'Rule Following', p. 73.
[23] Wright, *Wittgenstein on the Foundations of Mathematics*, p. 217.

Given that there is such-and-such a rule, then whether his doing so-and-so with the intention of following that rule *is* acting in accord with the rule depends only on what the rule is (just as given that a person has such-and-such an intention, then whether his intentionally doing thus-and-so in order to fulfil his intention *is* the execution of his intention depends only on what his intention is). Correctness and incorrectness are determined by the internal relation between the rule and what counts as accord with it. It is not a *discovery* that '1002' follows '1000' in the sequence of even integers. Rather, getting this result is a *criterion* for following the rule of this series.

What then of the person 'who falsely believes that he is conforming to a rule'? Is he merely 'disposed to think that certain cases fall under such-and-such a rule and others do not'? We must distinguish. One kind of case involves the agent's intending to follow the rule which stipulates that φing is required. The agent believes that following this rule consists in φing; and now he ψs, in the false belief that he has φd. This is an unproblematic case of mistake; it is typically recognizable by the agent and, at least sometimes, open to correction by him off his own bat. Certainly his thinking that he is following the rule and his following the rule do *not* collapse into each other. The second kind of case involves the agent's believing that the rule governing activity A in such-and-such circumstances requires one to φ, whereas it in fact requires one to ψ (e.g. he believes that the chess king, when checked, must move two squares). So whenever such circumstances arise he φs. Here he is mistaken over what the rule is; or he is simply following a *different* rule. And accordingly has a different concept of A-ing. (So he is not playing chess, but a variant of the game peculiar to him.) But again, he can and does distinguish between acting in accord with his rule that requires φing and contravening it.

The rule-sceptic may think this unfair. How does this 'rule-follower considered in isolation' know *which* rule he is following? For what the above reply suggests is that given that he is following or intending to follow the rule (or instruction) 'Add 2', then writing '1002' after '1000' is indeed predetermined as correct; for writing anything else will be incorrect. But how is this Robinson Crusoe to know which rule he is following? How can he 'remain faithful to the dictates of his understanding'? How can he be sure that he has understood the rule correctly?

This is scepticism run amok! The question 'How do you know what you mean by ". . ."?' is as awry as 'How do you know what you expect to happen?' or 'How do you know what you intend to do?' If the question is: 'What do you mean by "W"?', then it is fully answered by an explanation of meaning (hence without any reference to any community[24]). If the question is 'Are you sure that you know what "W" means?' (or 'Are you sure that your explanation of what "W" means is correct?'), then it is typically (though not necessarily) answered by 'Yes, of course I know what "W" means! I speak English. I have used "W" innumerable times and heard it used innumerable times.' One's confidence in one's mastery of a technique which one displays daily rests on just that fact – that one displays it, exercises this skill, daily. And if 'W' is a word in a language which, as it happens, only Robinson Crusoe speaks, the case does not essentially differ. The question concerns one's certainty about one's possession of (the continuity of) an ability or skill. And inasmuch as one exercises the skill frequently, one is typically perfectly confident, and rightly so. There is no room here for a serious sceptical foothold.

The phrase 'to follow the dictates of one's understanding' wrongly suggests that *something* (other than the rule) determines how the rule is to be applied, viz. the agent's own *interpretation*. Moreover, it is a misleading way of conveying the fact that one is exercising a normative skill (one's understanding whispers no dictates in one's ear, nor does it crank the handle of any neural calculator). The rule-sceptic compounds

---

[24] Reference to a community would only enter if our concern was to correlate what the speaker means by 'W' with what others mean by 'W', on the supposition that it is a word in a shared language. Or, if our concern was to compare the speaker's concept W with analogous concepts expressed by words in our language.

confusion by suggesting that the only grounds I *could* possibly have for judging how to apply an expression 'in conformity with my understanding of it' consist in my past applications of that expression.[25] But to apply a rule-governed expression correctly is to apply it *in accord with the rule for its use*. 'In accord with my understanding' is a misleading way of saying 'in accord with what I understand by it'. The very question of what is involved in my applying an expression in accord with what I understand by it is misleading in a context in which it is *evident* that I understand it correctly. For then what I understand by the expression *is* simply what it means. Be that as it may, what I understand by an expression is expressed by my answer to the question 'What do you understand by "W"?' (or 'What does "W" mean?'), i.e. by my explanation of the meaning of 'W'; and it is manifest in how I use 'W'. The suggestion that my past *applications* of a rule are the evidence that *I* must go on to 'discover' or 'determine' what I mean by 'W' (or what 'W' means), what I understand by 'W', or what rule for the use of 'W' I am now following, is surely absurd. (As absurd as the suggestion that my past behaviour in executing my past intentions to φ is evidence that I must rely on to determine what I now intend to do in intending to φ.) For there is no such thing as my having evidence or grounds for my now meaning such-and-such by 'W'. Understanding words (a language) is mastery of a technique, a skill, a capacity. In so far as a technique is characterized by rules, the question whether one possesses such a mastery must take the *content* of the rules to be fixed (not open). And the supposition that one might find oneself in the position of saying 'I understand something, but what on earth is it?' is absurd. Hence too, it is misguided to suggest that we know *what the skill that we have is* by scrutinizing past performances. Rather do we exhibit that skill by correctly explaining and correctly using the expression in question. Indeed, if I had to view my past uses of a sign as evidence from which to infer what rule I was following, then I

[25] Cf. Wright, *Wittgenstein on the Foundations of Mathematics*, p. 218.

could *not* see those past uses as meaningful. I would have to view them 'from an external point of view', as odd noises, curious inscriptions possibly governed by an as yet unknown rule. But I can no more view my own speech as evacuated of any meaning than I can view the ceiling of the Sistine Chapel as covered with meaningless blotches of paint.

All this might be conceded, and yet the rule-sceptic might still insist that the solitary rule-follower cannot distinguish seeming from being, thinking that he is following a rule from following one. But this is false, just as it would be false to suggest that I can never distinguish something's merely appearing thus-and-so to me from its being thus-and-so. It is an illusion that Robinson Crusoe must, as it were, be an idealist until the advent of Man Friday. If, when drunk, Crusoe plays patience ('Solitaire'!) and, putting down two red cards instead of one, thinks that the game has come out, then he is under the illusion that he has followed the rules of the game. And when he wakes up in the morning and looks at the cards left on the table, he will realize, just as you or I would, that he has broken the rules. How does he know that the rules of patience do not dictate 'When drunk, put down two red cards . . .'? How does he know that last night he was not playing such a version of patience? Exactly as anyone else knows or would know! That is not what he calls 'patience'. That is not what he calls 'a correct move'. And that is not how he plays the game or how he intended to play last night. It would be as wrong to think that it is only by reference to other people's rule-following that I can discern my seeming to follow a rule from my actually following one as it would be to think that I can only discern something's seeming to be two feet long, yet not being so, by reference to the measurements taken by other people.

5   Justification comes to an end

The previous reflections are intended to instil a modicum of scepticism about the schematic solutions to the apparent sceptical problems. Reversing our tracks, we shall now work backwards from the unsatisfactory conclusion through the reasoning which led to it. Although we ultimately aim to undermine the initial premises of the argument, we shall start by examining two of the intermediate conclusions. The first concerns the terminus of justification.

In following a rule, what I do is always the same. In expanding the series of even integers I always add 2, neither more nor less. Writing '1002' after '1000' is what I call 'doing the same' to 1000 as I previously did to 998, and indeed to every other term in the series. But, Wittgenstein insisted, I have no reason. I cannot justify calling this 'the same' by reference to further grounds. The rule-sceptic is fascinated by the terminus of justification, and prone to think that when 'I have reached bedrock, and my spade is turned'[26] then the whole panoply of rules, language and rule-following rests upon irrationality. The sceptic can always push one to the limits of justification *and beyond*. Thus Kripke, in setting up the sceptical problem, contends:

> It is tempting to answer the sceptic by appealing from one rule to another more 'basic' rule. But the sceptical move can be repeated at the more 'basic' level also. Eventually the process must stop – "justifications come to an end somewhere" – and I am left with a rule which is completely unreduced to any other. How can I justify my present application of such a rule, when a sceptic could easily interpret it so as to yield any of an indefinite number of other results? It seems that my application of it is an unjustified stab in the dark. I apply the rule *blindly*.[27]

And it may seem, to proponents of the community view, that wisdom lies in the recognition of necessity, that an unjustified stab in the dark is unobjectionable as long as it is made in good

---

[26] Wittgenstein, *Philosophical Investigations*, §217.
[27] Kripke, *Wittgenstein*, p. 17.

company. For as long as we all do it in the same way, 'no one will feel justified in calling the answer wrong'.[28]

This is confused. The supposition that the sceptic can rationally outstrip my justifications is false. What Wittgenstein says is 'If I have exhausted the justifications I have reached bedrock'. But 'exhausting the justifications' does not mean: having no justifications. It means: having run through them all. When I have spent my last penny paying off all my debts, it is true that I have no money left. But it is also true that I have no more debts! If I am asked what an expression means, I can explain it. An explanation of meaning is a norm of correct use. If my explanation is not understood, I can clarify it, i.e. I can give a further explanation of my explanation (a rule for the application of the rule). Ultimately, perhaps, I will explain by giving a series of examples with an 'and so on' rider. *This too is an expression of the rule*. Now my explanations will terminate at the point of showing that *this* and *this* . . . is what I call 'going on the same'. If I am *now* asked 'Why?', I can only say 'This is simply what I do'.[29] I have no *further* justification. But I have given a justification for what I do, so I cannot be accused of having made a stab in the dark.

The rule-sceptic concludes from my having no further justification that a justification is *missing*. He presupposes that my citing a rule does not justify what I do unless I can give a further justification for taking this rule to justify this action. *Pari passu*, I need a justification for taking this further justification to justify this conclusion – and so on. This is doubly incoherent. First, it generates a vicious infinite regress. Hence, according to this conception there is no such thing as a justification at all. Consequently there is nothing which my application of the rule could intelligibly be convicted of lacking. Secondly, it transgresses the bounds of sense. For in many cases the explanation for the fact that this statement (rule, formula, etc.) justifies acting thus is that this connection is part

[28] Ibid., p. 112.
[29] Wittgenstein, *Philosophical Investigations*, §217.

of the *concept* of justification. When, for example, I justify the claim that $68 \times 57 = 3876$ by producing the calculation

$$\begin{array}{r} 68 \\ \times\ 57 \\ \hline 3400 \\ 476 \\ \hline 3876 \end{array}$$

then the proper reply to the question 'What justifies taking this calculation as a justification (proof) of that equality?' is surely, 'Such calculations are what is *called* "justifications" in respect of such arithmetical equations'. Somebody who queries this connection does not exhibit an admirable caution about jumping to conclusions but rather betrays lack of grasp of the concept of justification. *Here* there is no such thing as *justifying* taking one thing to justify another.

Absence of grounds is a criticism if grounds are at least possible, and if doubt about justification is reasonable. But neither of these conditions obtains here, where justifications terminate. Precisely because a rule and its extension are internally related, because this nexus is grammatical, there can be no such thing as justifying it. For there is no such thing as justifying grammatical, conceptual connections by reference to reality. Absence of justification here does not betoken absence of something that *could* be present but is not. Hence it is no defect. Writing '1002, 1004, . . .' after '1000' in the course of expanding the series of even integers is internally related to the rule of the series '+ 2'. Writing anything else would not be following *that* rule correctly. That is what we call 'Adding two', that defines the series of even numbers. That *Fa* follows from *(x)Fx* is not something that admits of justification since that nexus is grammatical – that is what we call 'a sound inference'. What *justifies* calling rubies 'red'? Red is this ↑ colour; and rubies are this ↑ colour, i.e. red! Saying 'rubies are red' is a correct application of this rule for the use of 'red'. What *makes* it correct? Nothing. That is what we call 'applying "red" correctly'. There is no room for justification.

And as there is no room for justification, so too there is no room for genuine doubt. There is no such thing as doubting that *Fa* follows from *(x)Fx*, precisely because this is a grammatical connection. Since there is no such thing as justifying or providing grounds to support the legitimacy of this inference (*pace* model-theoretic justifications of inference) there is no such thing as querying whether it rests on adequate grounds. Any expression of doubt ('I wonder whether the proposition that all men are mortal entails the proposition that Socrates is mortal', or 'I wonder whether 1002 follows 1000 in the series of even integers') betokens not genuine doubt or grounds for doubting (there is no such thing as doubting a norm), but only failure of understanding. Someone who announces that he is uncertain whether this poppy (viewed in broad daylight, etc.) is red is not in need of further evidence or factual information, but instruction in what it means to call something 'red'. He needs to master the technique of using the expression in accord with the rule for its use.

Wittgenstein's rhetorical remark 'I follow the rule blindly', quoted out of context, suggests that normative behaviour is irrational, or non-rational. But in context it signifies not the blindness of ignorance, but the blindness of certitude. I know *exactly* what to do. I do not *choose*, after reflection and deliberation, I just ACT – in accord with the rule. The rule 'always tells us the same, and we do what it tells us',[30] 'we look to the rule for instruction and *do something*, without appealing to anything else for guidance',[31] 'it is my last court of appeal for the way I am to go',[32] 'I draw [its consequences] as a matter of course'.[33] On this confident exercise of normative skills, on the certain, unwavering understanding of what counts as following rules, are our language-games built. One follows rules blindly, but not mindlessly:

[30] Ibid., §223.
[31] Ibid., §228.
[32] Ibid., §230 (our translation).
[33] Ibid., §238.

One follows the rule *mechanically*. Hence one compares it to a mechanism.

"Mechanical" – that means: without thinking. But entirely without thinking? Without reflecting.[34]

The rule-sceptic falls victim to two related fallacies.[35] First, he hankers for grounds beneath grounds beneath grounds, in the belief that if there are no grounds supporting a ground then we have hit upon a form of irrationality. In the false belief that the philosophical task is always to *explain*, it seems to the rule-sceptic that where explanations (justifications) terminate irrationality takes over. Whereas the task is to *describe*. And the terminus of grammatical connections (chains of explanations) constitutes what we call 'rationality', for these connections *define* 'valid inference', 'counting', 'the number series', etc. Secondly, the rule-sceptic, while dissatisfied with the finitude of chains of reasons, never pauses to ask whether an 'infinite chain of reasons' would serve his purpose better. Would the rationality of our arithemetical, logical, etc. practices be sounder or clearer if the chain of reasons were interminable? Is there any such thing as 'an infinite chain of reasons'? Does not this absurd ideal rest on a misunderstanding? One must ask oneself what the function, the point, of giving grounds is. Would that point be served if one never reached the terminus of explanation with the remark: 'This is just what we *call* "doing such-and-such" ' ('checkmate', 'adding 2', 'specifying the colour', etc.)?

The platitude that every justification comes to an end therefore provides no foothold for scepticism. That the sceptic could interpret a given rule 'so as to yield any of an indefinite number of other results' shows only that he could *misinterpret* it in innumerable ways. It does not show that my confident, unreflective application of it is 'an unjustified stab in the dark'.

[34] Wittgenstein, *Remarks on the Foundations of Mathematics*, 3rd edn, ed. G. H. von Wright, R. Rhees, G. E. M. Anscombe (Blackwell, Oxford, 1978), p. 422.
[35] Cf. Wittgenstein, MS 116, 128.

6　The pitfalls of novelty

Sceptical *Angst* about new cases is involved in the second intermediate conclusion that merits scrutiny. As Kripke puts it:

> One point is crucial to my 'grasp' of this rule [for addition]. Although I myself have computed only finitely many sums in the past, the rule determines my answer for indefinitely many new sums that I have never previously considered. This is the whole point of the notion that in learning to add I grasp a rule: my past intentions regarding addition determine a unique answer for indefinitely many new cases in the future.[36]

On the background of this supposition, the rule-sceptic generates an anxiety neurosis about applying rules in the future. On this conception one has, in the last analysis, only a segment of the extension of the rule to guide one, i.e. one's own past applications of it. For any rule-formulation can be variously interpreted, and the only guide anyone has for how it is interpreted is precedent in his behaviour. But how can these precedents (past applications) guide one in new applications of '+2'? How can the expansion of the series '2, 4, 6, 8 . . .' up to '1000' tell one what to do beyond '1000', if, *ex hypothesi*, one has never reached beyond '1000' before? How do my past applications of 'red' show me whether to apply 'red' to this rose, which I have never seen before? For, the rule-sceptic argues, perhaps, in the past, by 'red' I always meant 'gred',[37] by 'addition' I always meant 'quaddition', and so on. Or, putting scepticism about what I meant to one side, the rule-sceptic may agree that, of course, by '+' I mean addition, but

[36] Kripke, *Wittgenstein*, pp. 7f.
[37] A Goodmanian term meaning, say, red until today and green henceforth.

how does, how *can*, the rule for addition guide me in applying 'addition' to new cases?

Many people become mesmerized by this patter about new cases, failing to notice the prestidigitations by which this sceptical conjuring trick is effected. But what determines whether an application of a rule is novel or not? *Ex hypothesi*, 1000 is a number to which I have never added 2 before; this flower is one I have never seen before. But does that make application of the rule a new application? Or a new kind of application? Is it not the case that, as Wittgenstein puts it, when I apply a rule, I apply it under the guise of 'Always the same'? If I said yesterday that my curtains are red, is predicating 'red' of my curtains *today* a new application? (After all, I have never said before that my curtains are red on 31 May 1983.) No, clearly not. This is applying the same rule *in the same way*. But is applying 'red' to this poppy, which I have never seen before, a new predication, a new use of 'red', or a new application of the rule (the ostensive explanation) for the use of 'red'? No. This ↑ [pointing to a sample] is red, my curtains are this ↑ colour, and this poppy is this ↑ colour. The rule is applied in the same way. That is what is called 'being red'. *Pari passu*, adding 2 to 1000 to yield 1002 is not doing something different to 1000 from what one does in adding 2 to 900 to yield 902. This is what is called 'adding 2'. This, relative to the series '+2', is called 'going on in the same way'.

The rule-sceptic thinks that what counts as doing the same thing is determined here by precedent. And he cannot see how to extract from precedent what 'doing the same' to a new case would be. In fact, what 'doing the same' is is determined by the rule. It is fixed by the technique of application of the rule, which is exhibited (typically) in the regular practice of following the rule. One cannot grasp a rule without knowing what it determines as doing the same, nor can one grasp the normative identity in a sequence of different acts (saying successively '1000', '1002', '1004' . . .) without grasping the rule with which they accord (each act consists in adding 2). So even though, *ex hypothesi*, I have never added 2 to 1000, writing

'1002' *is* going on in the same way as before, doing the same as hitherto. It is no more a novel ('unprecedented') application of the rule for addition than calling a hitherto unseen red object 'red' is a novel ('unprecedented') application of the rule for the use of 'red'.

Following a rule is a *Praxis*, a regular activity. One's understanding of a (rule-governed) expression is ultimately exhibited in its *application*, in *action*. For the mastery of the technique of using an expression in accord with a rule is a skill or capacity. Capacities in general, *a fortiori* normative capacities, are manifest in behaviour. Normative capacities involve the *use* of rules, in teaching, explaining, justifying, and correcting. It is the technique of employing a rule as a standard of correctness which determines what counts as doing the same. Measuring the lengths of objects which one has never measured before is *not* applying the rule for the use of 'metre' in a new way. One lays down the rule alongside the new object in exactly the *same* way as hitherto. This is what is called 'measuring'. (But measuring the distance to the moon *is* applying concepts of measurement in a new way!) The point of the notion that in learning to add I grasp a rule is not that the rule mysteriously determines a unique answer for indefinitely many *new* cases in the future (let alone that my intentions do). Rather should we say that the point is that it is of the nature of stipulating rules that future cases (typically) *are old cases*, that each application of a rule is doing the same again.

7   The roots of rule-scepticism

The previous two sections should encourage us in our distrust of the rule-sceptic, and induce us to go back to the beginning of his argument in the hope of discerning the legerdemain that led us credulously into sceptical confusion. The manner in which the sceptical problem was set up is in fact bogus. The allegation was that in our untutored and muddled way we think of ourselves as acquiring concepts (e.g. learning to add) by grasping rules. But which rule it is that we have grasped is something that needs to be determined by evidence. It is an open question whether 'plus', as I used the term in the past, denoted addition or something else, such as 'quaddition'. And my past uses of the term do not suffice to determine whether I used 'plus' with the intention of denoting the one function or the other.

No doubt it is harmless enough to say that I used 'plus' to *denote* addition. I not only intended to do so, I did do so. And that I did so was not determined by my *intentions*, but by the fact that 'plus' does denote addition. But this is a misleading way of saying that I used 'plus' correctly, in accord with its meaning. The metaphysical *Angst* that maybe 'plus', as I intended to use it, denoted not addition but quaddition, is an equally misleading way of suggesting that perhaps I used 'plus' in accord with the rule 'x plus y = the sum of x and y if x, $y < 57$, and otherwise = 5'. But what grounds are there for this anxiety? Did I ever explain 'plus' thus? Was it ever so explained to me? Was I ever taught that 'adding' meant going on in this bizarre way? Surely not. If 'Add 2' meant 'add 2 up to 1000, 4 from 1000 to 2000, 6 from 2000 to 3000, etc.', then 'Add 2' would not be correctly explained by '0, 2, 4, 6, 8, and so on'. There is no more reason for anxiety about addition or about the rule of the series of even integers than there is reason for thinking that as I used 'red' in the past it meant 'red until today, and green from today onwards'.

The appeal to the divide between past uses and future uses is likewise misleading. It subtly conflates questions about meaning and correctness of application of rules on the one hand with questions about ability and the continuity of an ability on the other. Whether acting thus-and-so (writing '. . . 1002, 1004, 1006 . . .') is a correct application of a given rule has nothing to do with my past intentions or with what I meant in the past, but only with the rule. That acting thus is correct is an aspect of the internal relation between the rule and its extension. Writing '. . . 1002, 1004, . . .' in compliance with the order 'Expand the series +2' is a *criterion* for following this instruction. Writing anything else would be a mistake. This has nothing to do with the past. On the other hand, evidence for whether a person has an ability, and hence, more specifically, for whether he has mastered the technique of using an expression in accord with a rule, is given by his performances, past and present. These constitute the criteria for the possession of the ability, and, more specifically, for understanding. But the fact that the evidence establishing possession of a capacity is past (or present) does not make questions about subsequent possession and exercise of those capacities open. For it is illegitimate to suggest that all that previous performances establish is previous possession of the ability, but that one can never tell whether one still has it.

The temptation to indulge in that sceptical ploy stems from an inclination to think of understanding or meaning something as *states of mind.* Mental states, unlike meaning and understanding, are actualities, not potentialities. And the continuity of a mental state is as unlike the continuity of understanding as the continuity of a fire is unlike the continuity of the combustibility of some straw. Mental states are interrupted (e.g. by sleep, or incompatible mental states or experiences). Understanding, mastery of a technique, cannot be thus interrupted, only lost or forgotten. As long as one thinks that one's past applications of a rule for the use of an expression are evidence for a *state* of meaning or understanding such-and-such by 'W', then it will remain an open question what one now means or understands by 'W'. The fact that I thumped on the table yesterday may show that I was angry yesterday (was in a 'state of anger'). But it goes no way to showing what my present state of mind is. So past evidence for yesterday's 'state of meaning' or 'state of understanding' cannot determine today's 'state'. However, understanding, mastery of a technique, is not a state but is rather akin to an ability. And the evidence of recent performances establishes not only that I had the ability when I did so-and-so, but that I *have* it. And the relation of an ability to time is unlike that of a state to time. If evidence establishes that I have mastered a technique, then it establishes not only that when I did . . . I was able, but rather that I am able. The suggestion that tomorrow I may not be able is one that needs evidential support. The past dissolvings of sugar establish not that sugar *was* soluble, but that it *is* soluble. Though human abilities differ from natural powers, my past calculatings establish not just that I could add, but that I *can* add (*ceteris paribus*).

A further source of confusion generating scepticism is the intrusion of anthropologism into the debate. Reflecting on the anthropologist's task of coming to understand the normative behaviour, including speech, of an alien society, we are readily led to the view that his task, like that of the physicist, is one of extrapolating an hypothesis from available data. The data consist of observed instances of normative conduct, the hypothesis is that the rule by which that conduct is governed is such-and-such. And just as the physicist's hypothesis is under-determined by the data, so too is the anthropologist's. For a finite array of applications can be mapped on to indefinitely many rules. But 'radical translation begins at home'. My position with respect to others resembles that of the anthro-pologist with respect to the alien tribe. Indeed, my initial learning of my native tongue was, it is held, a matter of wonderful childish inductive extrapolations from the be-haviour of others to the general rules they were following and which I was supposed to learn.[38] And finally, the sceptic proclaims triumphantly, my relationship to my own past is also like that of the anthropologist. In order to know what rules I am following, and what acts will conform to them, I must extrapolate from my past behaviour, and hypothesize the rule I have been following. All roads lead to rule-scepticism, and the only way out is via the sceptical solution of the community view.

[38] This supposition has induced Chomsky and his followers to weave incoherent fantasies about innate knowledge or cognition of a complex system of rules. See G. P. Baker and P. M. S. Hacker, *Language, Sense and Nonsense* (Blackwell, Oxford, 1984), chs 8–9.

But since, as we have seen, this alleged way out is blocked, we must back-track to see whether the correct way out was not passed right at the beginning of the journey. In the 'anthropological case' it is a mistake to think that the observer is given an array of normative acts, which he then has to correlate with a rule, *conceived as an explanatory hypothesis*. In the absence of the rule which is the standard of correctness, which stipulates what normative consequences doing so-and-so has, and by reference to which acting thus-and-so is called 'accord', all one has are not normative acts, but their empty vehicles, meaningless movements, noises, and inscriptions. Precisely because a rule and any part of its extension are internally related, it is absurd to think that one can determine solely from an array of acts *given non-normatively* what rule they fall under. The instruction: 'Observe A's behaviour throughout the day, and infer from that alone which acts were in conformity with orders given in the past!' is evidently absurd. As absurd, indeed, as 'Here is a man; now tell me who is his wife!'

Consequently, there is a complete disanalogy between the natural scientist's amalgam of empirical data with the explanatory hypotheses and the social scientist's endeavour to clarify normative behaviour. The observed physical phenomena the scientist seeks to explain and predict are *externally* related to the hypothesis the scientist constructs; the correctness of the identification of the phenomena is not necessarily vitiated by the falsification of the hypothesis. By contrast, the rule and the conforming behaviour are *internally* related. So too is *deviant behaviour*; for if behaviour is correctly identified as violating a rule, it confirms rather than falsifies the hypothesis *that there is* such-and-such a rule. A rule *is not an explanatory hypothesis*, although that a person or a community have such-and-such a rule may be. But to the extent that it is, that 'hypothesis' does not *explain* the behaviour in the sense in which a law of physics explains a natural phenomenon.[39] A

[39] Hence the correct but misleading contrast between explanation (*Erklärung*) in the physical sciences and understanding (*Verstehen*) in the social sciences.

rule for the use of an expression (e.g. '+' or 'red') is not a prediction about behaviour, but a standard of correctness. But, of course, that people have such-and-such rules must in general provide grounds for prediction.

A segment of the 'extension' of a rule *alone* will leave us in the lurch in our attempt at understanding what is being done. Merely knowing that people always write down '$42 \otimes 2 = 44$, $44 \otimes 2 = 46$', and so on will not provide grounds for inferring what '$\otimes$' means, since for all one can tell $50 \otimes 2$ may be 54 or 4 or anything one likes. Only in the context of complex patterns of behaviour would one be in a position to conjecture that these signs are rule-governed, let alone that they are a form of arithmetic. (After all, they might just be decorative patterns for murals.) And within the context of an appropriate 'form of life' what we (or anthropologists) ultimately need to confirm our conjectures about the meanings of the signs used, the normative acts performed, *is an expression of the rule (or rules), an explanation of meaning*. For what 'understanding' here consists in is a grasp of internal relations between rules and their applications, between rules and the concepts of 'doing the same', 'accord', 'following from the rule', and so on.

Of course, a rule-formulation is itself an array of signs; but it is an array of *meaningful* signs (hence there is no easy way of breaking into an alien language or culture). It can be variously interpreted, although only one set of equivalent interpretations will be correct. One must beware of misunderstandings here. First, the possibility of misinterpreting provides no grounds for sceptical worries that one has misinterpreted. Secondly, that a given rule-formulation can be misinterpreted does not signify that it is defective. Nor does it show that it is not a definitive explanation of the meaning (use) of the sign.[40] Thirdly, it is not the case that only giving interpretations shows whether one understands a rule, let alone that understanding a rule always involves interpreting it. *That* misconception Wittgenstein rejected with good reason. Although our

---

[40] Cf. Wright, *Wittgenstein on the Foundations of Mathematics*, p. 216.

understanding is manifest in the interpretations we may give, it is ultimately exhibited in our use of the expressions, our application of the rule in practice, in what we call 'following the rule' and what we call 'flouting it'. Hence, fourthly, it is not, of course, the mere rule-formulation, a certain form of words,[41] that mysteriously 'determines' such-and-such actions as correct. That thought leads directly to Platonism and scepticism. It is rather our practice of *using* the rule-formulation as an expression of a rule, as a canon of correctness, that constitutes the internal relation. Fifthly, whether a certain form of words, perhaps together with an action (e.g. of pointing) and an object (e.g. a sample) is or is not a rule-formulation is not determined by the *form* of words, but by the way in which it is used. Pointing at a rose and saying 'That is red' may in one context be an empirical statement, and in another an explanation of the meaning of 'red', a rule for the correct use of the word. '0, 2, 4, 6, 8, 10, and so on' may, in one context constitute applying the rule of the series '+ 2', in another an *explanation* of the rule; a rule-formulation, not an application. But, of course, not any form of words is used as a formulation of any rule. A blue sample is not used to explain what 'red' means (since to be red is *not* to be the colour of that sample), and '0, 5, 10, 15 and so on' is not used as a formulation of the rule of the series '+ 2' (since writing '20, 22, 24, 26 . . .' is *not* going on in the same way as '0, 5, 10, 15 and so on').

Finally, let us look again at the question which sent us off on this circuitous and futile journey: How does a rule *determine* what is in accord with it? The question presupposes that there are two autonomous things, the rule and (parts of) its extension. And we are called upon to discover what relates the two, what makes *these* actions and no others accord with the rule.

---

[41] It is, of course, quite wrong (a nominalist malaise) to think that a rule-formulation is a 'mere form of words'. This is just as misleading as the claim that a painting is a *mere* concatenation of blobs of paint (in which case it may indeed seem mysterious how one can have any notion of what a given picture depicts). To identify a symbol as a rule-formulation is, other things being equal, to recognize an internal relation between it and certain actions.

Platonism postulates abstract entities which, of their own accord, determine such consequences. But this is less of an explanation than a picture – which achieves nothing. The problem with it is, what does it mean? (And leniently viewed, one might say that it means that the rule and its extension are internally related.) Psychologism postulates magical acts of meaning. But that is to wrap a puzzle in an enigma. So we are inclined to fall back on the idea that an *interpretation* mediates between the rule and what accords with it. And the rule-sceptic correctly insists that with *these* assumptions[42] no one's interpretation can ward off corrosive doubt. But the sceptical solution does not fare any better. Perhaps the quest for an answer to this question was misguided *ab initio*. Should we not be looking at the question rather than looking for an answer?

The question presupposes that there are two independent things, the rule and its extension. These stand in a certain relation, namely that the latter is *in accord with* the former. And the problem posed was what is it that determines that relation-ship? Why are just these acts and not some others in accord with the rule? How can an object like a rule determine the infinite array of acts that accord with it? And how is it that when one understands a rule one grasps what acts accord with it? It should by now be evident that all these questions rest on a tacit, inchoate assumption that the relation between a rule and what constitutes acting in accord with it is *external*. Further, it is assumed that to *determine* such-and-such acts or applications as being in accord with the rule is an *external* property of whatever it is that does so determine these consequences. Implicit in the sceptical approach is the presumption that

---

[42] Bearing in mind the bizarre sceptical assumption that *because* when I give the instruction 'Expand the series +2', I do not *think* of '1002, 1004, . . .' or '20002, 20004, . . .' (and even if God were to peer into my mind He would not see those segments of the expansion there) *therefore* I do not mean or intend the pupil to continue thus (cf. Kripke, *Wittgenstein*, pp. 49ff.). This is the exact converse of the truth (and also of Wittgenstein's argument). *Of course*, when I order someone to expand the series of even integers I mean or intend him to write these numbers down! This *is* (part of) that series.

something, in this sense, determines that '1002, 1004 . . .' is the continuation past 1000 of the series of even integers, or that calling rubies 'red' is a correct application of the rule for the use of 'red' (a correct use of 'red'). Hence, it must make sense to ask *how* this is determined. And since an entity like a rule does not have the power to determine anything – understood as an *external* relation, and since there is no conceivable mechanism whereby it might do so (save in Platonist mythology) then something else *must* do so! Perhaps the mind; or perhaps an interpretation; or perhaps community dispositions to behave in certain ways. Yet the correct answer is that *in this sense*, nothing determines this. For it is an internal, not an external, relation. If '1002, 1004 . . .' were not part of the extension of the rule 'Add 2', then 'Add 2' would not be the rule it is. It is inconceivable that *this* rule have anything other than these applications as what constitutes accord with it. Similarly, given the rule for the use of 'red' (an ostensive definition by reference to a sample), and given that rubies are *this* colour, it is unthinkable that it should be an incorrect use of 'red' to say 'These are red'. It seems as if there are two independent things, the rule and its applications. In fact, they are two sides of the same coin. One can, of course, say that the rule determines such-and-such as its correct application at this point.[43] But then, not as an external property of the rule, and so not as an *explanation* of why *this* is a correct application of the rule. And so too, the question: '*How* does the rule determine this as its application?' makes no more sense than: 'How does this side of the coin determine the other side as its obverse?' Consequently, in understanding a rule one does not, as it were, first grasp the rule, and then look around to discover what accords with it. Rather, to grasp a rule is to be able to say what accords with it. There are not two separate operations of understanding, only one – an ability to judge that *this* and *this* and *this* accord with the rule that . . .

The extensive investigations into rule-scepticism and the

---

[43] Cf. Wittgenstein, *Philosophical Investigations*, §189.

various solutions to the apparent sceptical predicament lead into the wastelands of nonsense. Once that path is taken, the mirages of philosophical myth-making are unavoidable. And it costs more labour to emerge from these desert wastes than to enter them. As so often in philosophy, many a long and weary journey leads one, *if one is fortunate*, back to where one started. *To Nonsense and Back Again* might serve as the title of the report on this philosophical exploration.

3

Rule–scepticism and the harmony between language and reality

1 Scepticism and internal relations

Standard forms of philosophical scepticism can be traced to misapprehensions of conceptual articulations and misunderstandings of concepts. Wittgenstein's discussions of familiar forms of scepticism identified such sources of confusion. He argued that scepticism about the past stemmed from confusing the accompaniments of remembering with apparent grounds for making memory statements, and from wrongly divorcing the concept of the past from the concept of memory. He urged that scepticism about the 'external world' depended on conflating perceptions with sensations, and on mistakenly supposing descriptions of experience to be intelligible independently of descriptions of objects of experience. He diagnosed scepticism about other minds as rooted in misapprehension of the conceptual connections between psychological concepts and descriptions of behaviour, and in conceiving of first-person present-tense psychological utterances as descriptions of observed inner states or processes. In all such cases, misunderstandings of internal relations are the high-road to the confusions of scepticism.

The misunderstandings are multiple and ramifying. One deeply rooted misconception of the sceptic consists in searching for grounds supporting what is in effect an internal relation. He looks at what are called grounds for saying that a person is angry, and demands *further grounds for taking these grounds* to support the statement that this person is angry. Wittgenstein anatomized in detail this source of sceptical misconception. What counts *a priori* as grounds for or proof of a proposition is laid down in grammar. And it is a cardinal principle of Wittgenstein's philosophy that there is no such thing as justifying grammar by reference to reality.[1] Grammar (logic) is antecedent to truth. It delimits the bounds of sense; hence any description of reality put forward to justify grammar presupposes the grammatical rules. And since *nothing* lies beyond the bounds of sense but nonsense, then its 'description' cannot justify drawing the boundaries thus. Grammar is autonomous. Hence sceptical doubt about whether what is laid down in grammar as grounds for a proposition are really adequate grounds is not merely unjustified, it is literally senseless. For a denial that such-and-such is a ground disrupts an internal relation, and hence robs the allegedly doubtful proposition of (part of) its meaning. Hence it is no longer clear *what it is* that the sceptic doubts! Consequently there is no such thing as offering a general justification for taking propositions of this kind to make propositions of that kind certain, while the need to supplement a particular inference arises only against the background of a doubt which itself depends on grammatical stipulations that certain kinds of proposition count as evidence *against* the truth of a given proposition. General scepticism (but not well-grounded doubts in particular cases) betokens a variety of conceptual confusions.

This conclusion holds not only of traditional versions of scepticism, but also of the modern mutant *rule-scepticism*. It too depends on ignoring or distorting internal relations. And, although Wittgenstein did not explicitly address this monster as yet not conceived within the womb of philosophy, his discussion of rules and rule-following highlight the internal relations which rule-scepticism violates. Hence, as we have

---

[1] This crucial principle needs philosophical clarification and argument. It will be given on another occasion.

seen, one can readily extract from his writings a condemnation of the very point of view that he is wrongly taken to advocate. The further crucial tasks are to sketch additional aspects of the network of internal relations that centre on rules and to clarify what it means to speak of internal relations.

For clearing away the misconceptions of rule-scepticism, the important aspects of rules to note are those which confute the conclusions and premises of the sceptical arguments. One conclusion can be phrased in either of two ways: *either* it is impossible to be certain what rule anybody is following *or* it cannot be known how anybody will apply the rule he is following to novel cases (i.e. how he 'interprets' it). In the first version it is conceded that it may be certain that someone is following some rule; yet it is maintained that even if the agent states the rule that he is trying to follow, only experience can show what the content of this rule is since its content is inseparable from how it is applied. The substance of any rule is, as it were, a hypothetical construct from human actions. In the second version, the identity of the rule is divorced from its applications; what the rule is is one thing, what its applications are is another, and only an agent's independent interpretation links the two. Both of these routes converge on another conclusion: it cannot in general be known what accords with and what conflicts with the rule that a person is following. Indeed, it seems, there is no such thing as accord or conflict. For either there is no determinate rule that he is following, or novel applications of the rule turn on something external to the rule (viz. his interpretation of it). The rule that an agent intends to follow does not divide the logical space of possible actions into those that accord with it and those that conflict with it. Hence in many instances there is no possibility of objective knowledge about accord and conflict with a rule (and the 'community view' seems the only surrogate for objectivity).

This scepticism about what constitutes the correct application of a given rule is manifestly absurd. It presupposes the possibility of separating the grasp of a rule from knowledge of how to apply it. But to understand a rule *is* to know what acts count as correct applications and what acts as incorrect ones (or at least to know what considerations about an action would show it to be correct, and what would show it to be incorrect). It is widely held to be a conceptual truth that to understand a proposition is to know what would be the case if it were true. The parallel for rules is at least as plausible, namely that to understand a rule is to know what would count as acting in accord with it. What this truism rules out as unintelligible is the supposition that a rule can be grasped in ignorance of how it is to be applied. But this is precisely the supposition that the rule-sceptic seeks to justify. He purports to prove that for many rules, including all basic ones, understanding of a rule is coupled with very restricted knowledge of what its correct applications would be; certainty about the full range of its applications is in principle unattainable. In this way the rule-sceptic comes into conflict with a conceptual truth expressing an internal relation between rules and their applications. The principle that to understand a rule is to know what would count as acting in accord with it allows of no general exceptions (though it must be so construed that it tolerates the existence of hard cases under understood rules). Rule-scepticism transgresses the bounds of sense in concluding that there is no scope for objective knowledge about accord and conflict with rules.

A second internal relation is misrepresented in arguments for rule-scepticism. The relation between an intentional act and a rule which is described by saying that in acting thus the agent *followed* this rule is conflated with the relation between an event and an hypothesis which is described by saying that this event is *explained* by this hypothesis. 'Implicit rules' are nothing but explanatory generalizations, and this apparently anodyne remark is in fact nonsensical if 'implicit rules' are considered to be a species of rules. There are two aspects to this conflation. The first is the assumption that an act which counts as following a rule and the rule which is followed must be represented within the framework of hypothetico-deductive explanation. In particular, the rule must be formulated as a generalization, and the act must be so characterized that its description is an instantiation of this generalization. Nothing else is acceptable. Labouring under this pervasive misconception, theorists refuse to acknowledge many rule-formulations as expressions of rules at all. They think that formulating a rule by a sample (e.g. 'This ↑ is red') or by a series of examples (e.g. '0, 1, 4, 9, 16, . . .') is hocus-pocus, that the real rule is merely gestured at but must be differently formulated (e.g. 'Anything resembling this ↑ is red'[2] or '$x_0 = 0$, $x_{n+1} = x_n + 2n - 1$'. Yet whether an expression formulates a rule depends not only on its form, but on how it is used. The generality essential to a rule need not be made explicit in its expression, but is manifested in the applications of the rule-formulation. Rules, unlike hypothetico-deductive explanations, need not have the form of universal generalizations. The second misconception is the supposition that the rule that an agent is said to follow in acting thus-and-so may be as opaque to him as the received scientific explanation of some everyday process may be to someone who has the practical skill to carry it out (e.g. the chemistry of the action of yeast to a competent baker). It is true that in following a rule an agent need not rehearse the rule to himself at the time of acting. But this does not reduce rules to the status of conjectures. The rule followed must be known to the agent; he must be able to produce it (or relevant facets of it) if necessary, e.g. to justify his own behaviour. More accurately, the act that counts as following the rule must be intentional, and the intention must 'contain' the rule itself in the way that the rules of chess are related to the intention to play a game of chess. Clarifying this matter would be complex and full of subtleties. But what is crucial to note is independent of these details: there is nothing in the relation between an explanation and an explained event that corresponds to the restriction on what is admissible as a rule in characterizing an action as a case of following a particular rule.

[2] For analysis of this fallacy, see Baker and Hacker, *Wittgenstein: Understanding and Meaning* (Blackwell, Oxford, 1980), pp. 194ff.

A third internal relation is also distorted by rule-scepticism. It is assumed that an individual's behaviour is merely inductive or quasi-inductive evidence for his understanding a rule-formulation (or for what he understands by it). Indeed it is common to introduce the thesis that giving an interpretation is an intermediate step between understanding a rule and acting, and it is then argued that a person's actions are inductive evidence for how he interprets the rule-formulation. Such claims have a positive and a negative facet. The positive one is that a single act can definitely refute the claim that someone understands a rule (or interprets it thus). The negative one is that what a person understands by a rule (or how he interprets it) cannot be established with certainty. It is this which makes it an open question what he will count as acting in conformity with a rule that he seems to understand perfectly. The idea that how other people understand or interpret rules is essentially a conjectural matter is a manifestation of traditional scepticism about other minds. The notion that one must postulate one's own understanding on the basis of one's past behaviour rests on misconceptions about understanding and intentions that are peculiar to rule-scepticism. What these premises of rule-scepticism share is a failure to acknowledge that acting in certain ways (what is called 'acting in conformity with the rule') are *criteria* for understanding a rule, and that acting otherwise is a criterion for failing to understand it. This is precisely the point that Wittgenstein stresses in his response to the 'sceptical paradox' of *Philosophical Investigations*, §201; he observes that how someone understands a rule is manifested in his acting in the way that we call 'following the rule' and 'contravening it'. It is no more a mere hypothesis that someone who has successfully completed a certain training knows how to add than it is a conjecture that the pupil who continues the series '0, 2, 4, 6, . . .' with '1000, 1004, 1008, . . .' does *not* correctly understand the order to continue this series beyond 1000. In both cases something is conclusively established, even though it is conceivable that further evidence might upset the conclusion (and that yet further evidence might restore it!).

Understanding, though not an inner state, stands in need of outward criteria. The rule-sceptic distorts this internal relation between acts and rules by treating acting in accord with a rule as making understanding the rule merely a probable hypothesis.[3]

Each of these three important internal connections between rules and their applications is slighted in rule-scepticism. In fact, the problem with the rule-sceptic is not that he loses sight of them altogether, but rather that he pays attention to them intermittently. This is most clear if he adopts the view that rule-formulations are related to judgments of correctness only via interpretations. Here a free-wheel is inserted between a rule and its correct application, and this obviously removes any possibility of correctly understanding the idea that accord is an internal relation of acts with rules. Yet it is presumed that accord is an internal relation between acts and specific interpretations of rules and that acting in a certain way definitely settles (part of) an agent's interpretation of a rule-formulation. How is this possible? It seems that an interpretation can be expressed. But its expression will be another rule-formulation. Hence, *ex hypothesi*, it cannot alone settle what acts are in accord with it, but must be supplemented by a further interpretation. The upshot of this argument is that interpretations have an essential role in mediating between rules and their applications only if some rule-formulations alone determine what counts as accord. The rule-sceptic's idea is self-contradictory. In effect he alternately affirms and denies an internal connection between rules and their applications. He

[3] A recent perspicuous statement of this view (quite independently of rule-scepticism) is to be found in J. M. E. Moravcsik's 'Can There be a Science of Thought?': 'Suppose that all of the relevant behavioural signs such as reaction to the sentence under various circumstances, the ability to manipulate the symbols involved in processes like paraphrase, and substitutions, etc. are positive. It remains a theoretical possibility that the agent does not understand the sentence and has merely acquired a convincing behavioural repertoire in terms of which he can "fake it" . . . There is no certainty in ascription of understanding, only probabilities' (*Conceptus*, XVII (1983), No. 40–41, p. 250).

does so again in maintaining that an agent's actions show a partial interpretation, whereas what he cannot do is to explain why any actions at all demonstrate anything (however weak) about how an agent understands a rule. The rule-sceptic helps himself to an internal connection between actions and understanding rules in the course of constructing an argument that there is no such connection!

The neglect of internal relations reveals not only the inconsistencies in the sceptic's reasoning, but also the full absurdity of his conclusion. He denies that it is possible to ascertain accord and conflict with a rule over the full range of its potential applications. This position could be reached by the following route. He would concede that to understand a rule is to know what acts would count as being in accord with it (and perhaps too what acts would count as being in conflict with it), but he would draw the conclusion from this that only experience will show what someone understands by a rule-formulation. For what he would count as accord with this rule can be established only by observation of his behaviour in trying to follow the rule (and perhaps too what he says about his own imagined behaviour or the actual behaviour of others). The content of the phrase 'what acts he would count as being in accord with the rule' must be ascertained by experiment, and prior to making any particular experiment we can only speculate about what the result might be. In this way, relating understanding a rule to what counts as its correct applications leads to the conclusion that the meaning of a rule-formulation can be ascertained only by experiment. This is a bizarre thesis. Exactly parallel reasoning would be applicable to the basic contention of truth-conditional semantics, namely that to understand a declarative sentence is to know what would be the case if it were true (and also what would be the case if it were false). Is it thought to follow from this platitude that any form of truth-conditional semantics must be an experimental theory of meaning? Are the truth-conditions of a sentence to be established by bringing it about that it (or what it expresses) is true and then investigating what happens to be true in such circumstances? Many philosophers would rightly balk at these absurd implications. What a sentence expresses is held to be its truth-conditions; hence the supposition that what it expresses is true is the supposition that its truth-conditions are fulfilled, and this eliminates the possibility of any experimental investigation of truth-conditions on the supposition that the sentence is true. Do parallel objections not hold against ascertaining the meaning of a rule-formulation by experiment? Whether somebody who, *ex hypothesi*, understands a rule knows what acts would be in conformity with it, even whether he would count *this* act as correct, *that* one as incorrect, are not meant as expressions of hypotheses to be confirmed or disconfirmed by his future behaviour; they are alternative formulations of the claim that he understands the rule. Anybody who understands the principles of arithmetic would count $57 + 75 = 132$ as a correct step of addition; and hence with perfect propriety and in the absence of experimental confirmation, we would say of Einstein that he would have counted this sum as correct. The counterfactual supposition that such a person would count *this* act as in accord with the rule is misconceived if it is thought to need (or to be strengthened by) direct experimental confirmation. But this misconception is integral to the position of the rule-sceptic. For otherwise the unlimitedness of the range of acts that a person would count as in accord with a given rule would not supply any grounds for scepticism, but simply reflect the unlimited applicability of the rule that he understands. Scepticism is no more the corollary of acknowledging that understanding a rule is inseparable from knowing how to apply it than it is a consequence of identifying understanding a declarative sentence with knowing what its truth-conditions are.

2   Internal relations and criteria

The diagnosis that rule-scepticism, like traditional forms of scepticism, arises from distortion of internal relations may be potentially illuminating, but the light that it sheds on these misconceptions will be no stronger than one's grasp of this notion of an internal relation. What exactly is the significance of characterizing accord as an internal relation between rules and actions? There is in fact a cluster of properties in virtue of which relations are classified as internal. In early writings Wittgenstein stressed two features of internal relations. One is that a relation between two entities is internal only if it is inconceivable that those two entities should not stand in this relation.[4] This point might be rephrased in various ways, e.g. that it is necessarily true or a tautology that these entities stand in this relation, that it would be self-contradictory to suppose that they did not do so, or that it is not a genuine question whether or not they do. The second feature, which Wittgenstein realized only later, is that an internal relation between two entities cannot be decomposed or analysed into a pair of relations with some independent third entity.[5] Nothing external to the two related entities can mediate between them, since this would make the existence of the internal relation dependent on the existence of a suitable third entity and its relations with each of the given pair of entities. Either that third entity is externally related to the relata of the internal relation, in which case the nature of the internal relation is distorted; or it is internally related to them, in which case it is redundant (*see below*). Both of these features are prominent in Wittgenstein's examples and discussions of internal relations.

One case repeatedly mentioned in his discussions in the early 1930s is the relation between a desire and its fulfilment. Wittgenstein castigated Russell's account[6] of desire according to which a conscious desire is a feeling of discomfort which causally generates a behaviour cycle that terminates in a condi-

[4] See, for example, Wittgenstein, *Tractatus Logico-Philosophicus* tr. D. F. Pears and B. F. McGuinness (Routledge and Kegan Paul, London, 1961), 4. 123.

[5] See, for example, D. Lee ed., *Wittgenstein's Lectures, Cambridge 1930–1932* (Blackwell, Oxford, 1980), p. 57.

[6] Russell, *Analysis of Mind* (Allen and Unwin, London, 1921), ch. 3.

tion of quiescence. The desire is said to be *for* the state of affairs that brings quiescence, and it is 'conscious' when accompanied by a true belief as to the state of affairs that *will* bring quiescence. Wittgenstein criticized this account on the ground that it excluded the element of intentionality from the characterization of desire.[7] To know that a state of affairs which is realized (or object that is presented) is the object of one's desire is to apprehend an internal relation. But on Russell's account it involves *recognition* that *this* is what one wanted. And this recognition of the realized object of desire is conceived as an external relation. This in effect makes it an open question whether what somebody sincerely *avows* to be the object of his desire really *is* so. Something quite different may bring about the feeling of quiescence. This will be 'recognized' when the avowed object of desire occurs. But this is absurd:

> I believe Russell's theory amounts to the following: if I give someone an order and I am happy with what he then does, then he has carried out my order. (If I wanted to eat an apple, and someone punched me in the stomach, taking away my appetite, then it was this punch that I originally wanted.)[8]

It is a necessary truth, or a truth of grammar, that the fulfilment of the desire to drink a pint of lager is drinking a pint of lager, not having a swim, let alone being punched in the stomach (even though the latter two events may lead to 'quiescence' of the desire). What is desired is not ascertained by experiment, but rather it can be read off the expression of the desire:

> Isn't it like this: my theory is completely expressed in the fact that the state of affairs satisfying the expectation of *p*

[7] Wittgenstein, *Philosophical Remarks*, ed. R. Rhees, tr. R. Hargreaves and R. White (Blackwell, Oxford, 1975), pp. 63ff.
[8] Ibid., p. 64.

is represented by the proposition *p*? And so, not by the description of a totally different event.⁹

The relation between a desire and its fulfilment is not mediated by a third thing, viz. a feeling of satisfaction which is recognition that the event produces quiescence and hence is what is desired. Rather, this relation is forged in language. A desire and its fulfilment make contact in grammar: from the expression of desire can be derived without more ado a description of what constitutes its fulfilment. The desire that *p is* the desire that is fulfilled by *p*; the expectation that it will rain *is* the expectation that is satisfied by its raining. Here are archetypal internal relations which, when not correctly apprehended, are a source of philosophical bafflement and confusion. In such cases as desire, expectation, orders, and wishes, Wittgenstein strove to exorcise the ghost of a third entity that philosophers are tempted to insert between the two terms of an internal relation (*see below*).

The relation of a desire to its fulfilment is a useful model of what Wittgenstein calls an 'internal relation', but not all of its features are replicated in every instance of an internal relation. In particular, Wittgenstein repudiated the implication that any expression of an internal relation must be a necessary truth or a tautology. He characterized the relation between an observation-statement and an hypothesis as internal or grammatical even though he explicitly asserted that neither the conjunction of the observation-statement with the negation of the hypothesis nor the conjunction of the hypothesis with the negation of the observation-statement were self-contradictory.¹⁰ Observations speak for or against hypotheses; they make hypotheses more or less probable. But that this is so is part of the grammar of hypotheses. There is an internal relation, for example, between such a macroscopic observation as a track in a cloud

⁹ Ibid., p. 66; the case of expectation runs exactly parallel to desire.
¹⁰ Wittgenstein, *Philosophical Remarks* ch. XXII.

chamber and the presence of a charged particle, since the one concept is *explained* in terms of the other.

The same point holds in respect of what he called 'criteria'. Acting in certain ways (e.g. moaning and holding an injured limb) is a criterion for being in pain. But the statement 'If someone acts thus, he is in pain' is *not* a tautology. One may be in pain yet not show it, and one may display pain-behaviour without being in pain. Criterial support is defeasible. Nevertheless, the relation between outward behaviour and an inner state which Wittgenstein expresses by saying that pain-behaviour is a criterion for being in pain is laid down in grammar. It is not derived from observation of pain-behaviour or from experiencing pain. Though not a tautology, the relation of pain-behaviour to pain is an internal relation. The fact that A's pain-behaviour in such-and-such circumstances justifies ascribing pain to him does not, *ceteris paribus*, need the support of any further investigation of human behaviour in general or of A's particular physiological or psychological condition. The fact that in certain *special* circumstances we may require further evidence (since defeating conditions obtain) does not show that in ordinary circumstances the justification for the judgment that A is in pain is incomplete or even that it is capable of non-trivial supplementation.

There is a further, slightly more complex, point of similarity between the kind of internal relation involved in this case, and the simpler kind exemplified by the relation of desire to its fulfilment. Pain avowals, utterances such as 'I am in pain', 'It hurts', are criteria for pain. Of course, they may be insincere, and evidence of insincerity defeats their criterial support. But if sincere, they support the judgment that the person is in pain. We are strongly inclined, however, to view a sincere avowal as a description of the speaker's inner state. He experiences a pain, we argue, he *recognizes* his experience *as* a pain, and then he puts it into words, saying 'I am in pain'. Here again philosophical reflection is prone to interpose a third entity, an act of recognition, in order to explain an internal relation. For it seems that his utterance 'I am in pain' is evidence (for us) that he is in pain because it is a report of something which he (and he alone) has recognized (since he has 'privileged access to it'). But this act of recognition, Wittgenstein contends in the private language argument, is a fiction. An avowal of pain is itself a form of *learnt* pain-behaviour, which no more rests on inner recognition than does a groan. Recognition does not mediate between pain and its expression, and the criterial support which an avowal of pain lends to a judgment that that person is in pain is determined by grammar. This internal relation does not rest on any third thing.

Philosophers have notoriously found difficulty in making sense of Wittgenstein's remarks about criteria. The crucial problem is to explain how an internal relation can be defeasible. Defeasibility amounts to the absence of any entailment, while an internal relation must be a necessary connection. Can there be necessary connections that fall short of entailment? Again, evidence is typically held to render a proposition certain if and only if it confers upon it the degree of probability of 1. But philosophers have commonly thought that only entailment confers the probability of 1 upon an hypothesis. Yet Wittgenstein suggests that undefeated criterial support renders the proposition supported certain. How can this be?

This is not an occasion for resolving these conundrums. *Pro tempore* the merest sketch must suffice. The cash-value of classing certain statements as necessary truths or as rules of grammar is to characterize their use. This has two distinctive facets. One is that such a statement has a particular role in such normative activities as teaching the use of expressions and in justifying and criticizing applications of expressions. The other is that these statements are *ex officio* immune to impeachment. Nothing counts as a legitimate challenge to a rule of grammar, and hence nothing qualifies as a justification of it. These characteristics of rules of grammar hold of certain statements that correspond to criterial relations. 'If somebody moans and holds his injured foot, then he is in pain' or 'People who act like *that* are in pain' can be used to justify the assertion that a particular person is in pain, and there is no such thing as a more basic general principle which we would take as justifying these statements. If challenged to produce grounds for them, one might well reply 'That is what pain involves' or 'I know what "pain" means'. These points hold *independently of the defeasibility* of the inference from pain-behaviour to pain. Defeasibility concerns the conditions under which we countenance a principle of inference and the conditions under which we judge its application to be unwarranted. But the fact that there are restrictions on the application of a rule of grammar does not alter the character of the rule that is applied when these conditions are met. Puzzlement about criteria arises from attempting to write into the formulation of every acknowledged rule of grammar the conditions under which it is applicable. But as long as these conditions are agreed and open to objective assessment, there is no need even to make this attempt.[11] That the relation between inner states and outward behaviour is internal is expressed in our taking, *ceteris paribus*, certain statements as the justification for judgments we make about states of mind; or perhaps in our making these judgments without conceding the need for supplementary premises. The restriction of internal relations to the content of statements which count as necessary truths or tautologies unduly narrows attention to a proper subset of statements that have the role of rules for the use of expressions. A wider conception is essential for making sense of the logic of natural languages, and a corresponding extension of the notion of an internal relation, though unorthodox, is illuminating.

It is against this background that the clarification of certain internal relations between rules and their applications must be understood, in particular the relation between understanding a rule and knowing how to apply it and the relation between understanding a rule and acting in conformity with it. Rule-scepticism feeds on two features of these internal relations.

---

[11] It may in many cases be futile or incoherent, especially in view of the fact that there is no such thing as a complete list of the conditions which defeat an inference based on the satisfaction of criteria.

The first is the defeasibility of their support for certain inferences. The sceptic is impressed by the fact that someone's general success in applying a given rule in the past (or in making correct judgments about the correctness of its applications) does not guarantee a correct understanding of the rule in the present or correct applications of this rule to future cases. The conformity of his actions with the rule might be a mere coincidence, and his judgments about correctness, though faultless in their conclusions, might be based on a systematic misunderstanding of the rule which would emerge only in future applications. The sceptic takes the defeasibility of those inferences to prove that doubt is rational, that there is no such thing as certainty that a person understands a rule correctly or no such thing as certainty that he knows how to apply it over the full range of its applicability on the basis of his satisfying conventional standards for understanding it.

The second thing that weighs with the rule-sceptic is that some of the internal relations between rules and their applications do not fit the model of the internal relation between a desire and its fulfilment. It might seem self-evident (or a tautology) that the rule that the king may not move through check in castling is complied with by not castling through check. Here the rule and its application seem to make contact in language since the formulation of the rule and the description of an act of complying with it largely overlap. But for more primitive rules this is not so. If it is supposed, e.g., that elementary arithmetical operations are taught only by examples and working exercises, then the rule for forming the series of even integers will be correctly applied at the 500th step only by someone who produces the sum of 2 and the 500th term. But whether 1000 is the sum of 2 and the 500th term (998) is just the same question as how the series is to be continued at this point. It seems that if this sum has not been explicitly mentioned in the training in addition, then the rule for continuing the series cannot be conceived to lay down explicitly what step is correct at this point. That '1000' is the 501st term in the series of even integers, i.e. that '1000' is the result of a correct application of the rule of the series '0, 2, 4, . . .' to the 500th term, cannot be dictated by a rule that is silent about this case. In respect of any such private rules, it seems what counts as a correct application in general cannot be considered to be internally related to this rule itself; the rule as it is formulated and judged to be understood must be supplemented in order to reach out to its unlimited range of applications.

The rule-sceptic's responses are intelligible but misguided. There is no cogent argument proving that the mere fact of defeasibility (the *possibility* of defeat) justifies doubt or the denial of certainty. The *presence* of defeating conditions justifies doubt, but the *intelligibility* (imaginability) of defeating conditions does not. The supposition that defeasibility justifies doubt is tantamount to the absurd proposal that possible doubt is a kind of doubt, that imaginable reasons for doubt in *other* circumstances are, in *these* circumstances here and now, actual reasons for doubting. Furthermore, doubt is only intelligible within an established framework of concepts, for *what it is* that is being doubted must stand firm. But the very concept of an ability is partly determined by the grammatical fact that such-and-such conditions (e.g. behaviour in certain circumstances) justify attributing that ability to a person. If this justificative nexus were served, then it would be wholly unclear what it is that is held to be doubtful. For that this internal relation obtains is an aspect of the concept of this ability. To call it into doubt is not to deny the apparent facts, but to disrupt the concept.

The apparent opacity of *some* of the internal relations between rules and their applications is a feature shared with other internal relations. Thus, for example, certain kinds of agitated behaviour in certain circumstances are familiar criteria for a person's being angry, but the descriptions of the behaviour and the sentence 'He is angry' have nothing in common apart from the reference to the person. They do not seem to make contact in language – or at least they do so (in the characterization 'He reacted angrily') only in virtue of the internal relation. But if they do not make contact in language on the perspicuous model of the characterization of desire and the characterization of its satisfaction, they make contact in the practice of using language, of explaining and justifying its use. So too here. The specification of the rule of the series of even integers made no mention of 1002 succeeding 1000, or of 20002 succeeding 20000. But to grasp what 'adding 2' means is to know that these numbers occur in the series. To understand the rule is to know what *counts*, in this technique, as *doing the same*. And these too are internal relations, even if not modelled on the paradigm of the relation of an expectation to its fulfilment.

A correct understanding of the internal relations between rules and their applications, and between understanding a rule and applying it correctly, robs rule-scepticism of its charms. Wittgenstein laboured to make clear the nature of these internal relations. He emphasized that behaviour is a *criterion* for possession of an ability, and, in the specific case of understanding rules, that how one applies a rule is a criterion for how one understands it. And he stressed that internal relations are not cemented together by third entities (in this case, by interpretations). It is ironic that he should be thought to steer philosophers in the direction of rule-scepticism (let alone to provide sceptical solutions for it) when in fact he sought to signpost the many pitfalls that are strewn across this highway to misunderstanding and nonsense.

3 The harmony between explanation and use

Philosophical Investigations §§185–242 highlights the internal relations between rules and their applications. It thereby provides the ammunition for sinking any form of rule-scepticism. Nonetheless to interpret these remarks as targeted on scepticism would be an anachronism. Wittgenstein did not concoct this hitherto unknown form of philosophical madness and then labour to destroy it. This leaves an apparent mystery.

What was the purpose of this central section of the *Investigations*? The rule-sceptical interpretation of these remarks gains much of its allure from the absence of any recognized alternative. Until its advent, this part of the *Investigations* was simply ignored. And if a concern with rule-scepticism is bundled off the stage, will this segment of the argumentative drama not once again be plunged into obscurity?

Incomprehension of the strategic purpose of Wittgenstein's general remarks on rules and following rules is a symptom of failure to grasp the contours of the preceding remarks and the whole drift of his earlier writings on the topic of meaning. The remedy is to take a wider look around.

The explicit focus of the opening part of the *Investigations* is what Wittgenstein called 'Augustine's picture of language'. This is the pre-theoretical conviction that words are names whose meanings are the objects named (and the corollary that sentences are mere combinations of names which function as descriptions of states of affairs). Wittgenstein thought this conception to inform the construction of theories of meaning by such philosophers as Frege, Russell, the author of the *Tractatus*, and Carnap, and no doubt he would have discerned its continued influence in modern semantic theories for natural languages. In his view, this climate of theory-construction produced little but fresh misunderstanding. Correlating words with things seems to be the key to the concept of meaning because it appears to make clear the essential nature of understanding expressions. But this is an illusion. Understanding is manifested in speech, in the use that a speaker makes of an expression and in the explanations he gives of what it means. To describe someone as having correlated a word with a particular thing says nothing by itself about how he uses this expression or how it is to be used; or rather, it will make these issues clear only on the assumption that everything about what the word means is understood apart from what it stands for (cf. *Philosophical Investigations*, §§30ff.). What the elucidation of the concept of meaning must articulate are just those matters taken for granted in elaborating theories on the basis of the Augustinian picture. It must be made clear what correlating a word with an entity amounts to *in the practice of speaking the language* (§51) and how a correlation sets up a standard of correctness for using a word.

Wittgenstein reorients the philosophical investigation of the concept of meaning by bringing to the forefront the concept of the use of a word and *explanations* of what it means. Using a word correctly is a criterion of understanding it (or, more generally, how it is used is a criterion of how it is understood). And explaining it correctly is also a criterion for understanding it (or how it is explained is a criterion for how it is understood). Hence the familiar slogans 'The meaning of a word is its use in the language' and 'The meaning of a word is what is explained in explaining its meaning'.

These ideas lead directly to an indictment of theories of meaning which embroider on the Augustinian picture of language. To know what a word stands for is alone insufficient to settle its use, whereas to know how to use a word renders superfluous the enquiry into what it stands for (and provides an answer to this question in cases where it makes sense). In the analysis of the concept of meaning, the relation of designation typically drops out. The parallel point about explanations of meaning is even more revolutionary. Philosophers have commonly thought that understanding transcends speakers' ability to give explanations of what they understand. Actual explanations, say by example, allegedly fail to capture the entire meaning of an expression (e.g. of 'game', 'number' or 'plant'), while ostensive definitions convey something that is altogether ineffable (e.g. the indefinable meaning of 'red' which is grasped only through acquaintance with a sensible property). And semantic theories are considered to be attempts to fill in the gap between what is understood and what is explained in 'everyday explanations of meaning'. Wittgenstein pulls the rug out from under this conception. What speakers understand is *completely* expressed by the explanations they can give (cf. §75); there is no gulf to be filled between understanding and everyday explanations of words; and hence, in so far as philosophy centres on the clarification of meanings, it must eschew all hypotheses and discoveries about what is hidden (cf. §§122ff.). To cut meaning down to the size of accepted explanations is to eliminate the logical space in which theories of meaning move and have their being.

These negative achievements are preliminaries to more constructive clarification of the crucial notions of understanding and explanation. This is the task inaugurated in §143 and carried on down to the end of the private language argument.

The concept of understanding is eclipsed, but not absent, in the Augustinian picture. It is clearly considered to boil down to a mental act of effecting a bond between a word and what it signifies. Correct intelligent speech must in some mysterious way be contained in and flow from instantaneous acts of associating words with things. Hence, if the Augustinian picture is misguided, this must be a total misconception of understanding. What then should replace it? Wittgenstein struggles to clarify this, exploiting the only admissible evidence, viz. reminders about how we use and explain the term 'understand'. The upshot of these investigations is that one of the supports of the Augustinian picture, namely that understanding is a mental act, state or process, is radically incoherent. Understanding closely resembles an ability, but is altogether unlike paradigmatic mental acts, states or processes. Making correct applications of a term is a criterion for understanding it, just as repeatedly hitting the bull's-eye is a criterion for having the capacity or skill of a good archer.

A second major task for Wittgenstein is to clarify the concept of explaining the meaning of an expression. Giving a correct everyday explanation of meaning is also a criterion of understanding. But philosophers are prone to distort or repudiate this internal relation. On the one hand they are inclined to dismiss common-or-garden explanations as incorrect or as not real explanations at all (e.g. an explanation of 'two' by ostensive definition[12]). Here they are mesmerized

[12] Note that Wittgenstein says of this humdrum explanation (viz. pointing at two nuts and saying 'The number of nuts is two' or 'That is two nuts')

by *bogus ideals* of explanation, as if a proper explanation must be incapable of being misunderstood, or must settle for every possible object whether it falls under the explained concept or not, and so on. And they are deluded by *forms* of explanation, thinking that only formal definitions are genuine explanations, even though we rarely employ such definitions in our practices of explaining or justifying our uses of words, and, in many cases, would not understand them, even though we have mastered the use of the expression thus 'explained' (e.g. 'two'). On the other hand, philosophers in the grip of the Augustinian picture are inclined to think that 'ultimately' explanations of expressions by definitions replacing one symbol by others must terminate in an array of 'indefinables'. These expressions, philosophers think, must somehow be *connected with reality*, for it is they that give content to the language. And the foundations of understanding apparently must lie in grasping the manner in which these expressions are connected with things. At this point, two complementary misconceptions are common. Typically ostensive definition, or some distorted surrogate of it (e.g. 'mental' or 'private' ostensive definition) is invoked to connect language with reality. Here the sample pointed at is taken to be part of what is represented rather than belonging to the means of representation. Secondly, the 'mechanism' of connecting language with reality is typically attributed to the mysterious workings of the mind. [13] What breathes life into dead signs must be the mind.

---

that it is 'perfectly exact' (*Philosophical Investigations* (Blackwell, Oxford, 1953), §28).

[13] This 'classical' conception has undergone an interesting transmutation since Wittgenstein's day. Explanation of 'indefinables' is a neglected issue, and contemporary theories of meaning are silent about ostensive definition. Rather, they hold that proper scientific explanations of meaning framed in an appropriate metalanguage themselves make connections between language and the world. This is (part of) the role of T-sentences. The nexus with understanding is correspondingly distorted: these metalinguistic statements are construed as hypotheses about the theory of meaning *tacitly known* by a speaker (or, more cautiously – and obscurely – as hypotheses about the

Meaning a symbol in a certain way, intending it to be understood thus and not otherwise, are mental acts essential to
intelligent discourse.

The fallacies involved in this apparently simple picture are
multiple and mutually reinforcing. Their exposure is taken for
granted in *Investigations* §§185ff. (having been discussed earlier
in the book, or in earlier writings). Here we mention only two
salient points.[14] First, in reflecting upon the nature of a
language and our understanding of it, we are prone to consider
signs in abstraction from their use. We then lose sight of the
fact that what makes a sound or mark a label, a house-number,
an order, a signpost, etc., is a pattern of use visible in the overt
activities of producing and responding to such signs. It is not
correlation with things in the world by means of a curious
mental mechanism that invests signs with their significance,
but the rule-governed potentiality for use and its corresponding realization in actual use. Appreciating this short-circuits
the appeal to the mental. Hence acting in appropriate ways in
producing or responding to an order, a rule, an avowal of pain,
a label, etc., is a criterion of understanding the signs
employed. Indeed, were this not conceded, there would be no
such things as signs at all – for it is *this*, not mental acts of
meaning, that gives them life. The second crucial point is that
whatever can be meant or intended must be capable of being
expressed. A person may know more about what he means
than he says, but not more than he can say or express. This
point was raised earlier in the *Investigations* (§75) and is the crux
of the private language argument. Mental acts of meaning do
not have the capacity by themselves to endow signs with
meanings (intelligible uses). Meaningfulness requires use in
accord with a standard of correctness, a rule. Such rules are

---

content of the ability to speak and understand a language). For detailed
analysis and criticism of these confusions, see Baker and Hacker, *Language,
Sense and Nonsense* (Blackwell, Oxford, 1984), chs 5–6, 8–9.

[14] For detailed criticism, see Baker and Hacker, *Wittgenstein: Understanding
and Meaning* (*passim*).

given by explanations of meaning. And concentrating one's attention, say, upon a mental image or sensation (in a 'private ostensive definition') does not provide a standard of correct use, neither a public one nor a private one. The removal of these misconceptions, however, is not the principal aim of §§185–242.

A third obvious task Wittgenstein undertakes is the over-arching strategic purpose of these central sections. In connecting the concept of meaning both with explanation and with use, Wittgenstein may seem to have done too much. He has apparently given *two* clarifications of a single concept. Still worse, it seems that those clarifications of 'meaning' are *independent* of each other. Surely somebody might explain a word correctly, but go on to use it mistakenly, perhaps even making frequent and systematic errors. So too a person might give the appearance of understanding an explanation given to him and yet misapply the defined word (e.g. mistaking an ostensive definition of a colour for an ostensive definition of a number or a direction). Conversely, a person who applies a word impeccably may produce an explanation of it which is manifestly incorrect or he may accept another's suggested explanation even though this is unacceptable and at odds with his own pattern of use. These possibilities seem to pose an embarrassing dilemma. By one standard such a person understands an expression correctly, by another standard he does not. The conflict, however, is only apparent, stemming from the assumption that the concept of explaining what a word means and the concept of using a word correctly are independent. Wittgenstein's purpose was to expose this misconception by making clear how explanation and use are internally related. In viewing an explanation of the meaning of a word as a rule, a standard for its correct use, and in viewing the uses of a word as applications of this rule (instances of following it), he conceived of the relation between explanation and use of a word as a special case of the relation between a rule and its applications. Hence clarification of the internal relations between rules and their applications is also a clarification of the internal relations between explanations of meaning and uses of words. This is precisely the programme executed in §§185–242. The widening of focus to include signposts, rules of chess, and master-patterns under the umbrella of clarification of the concept of a rule and rule-following should not blind a perceptive reader to the fact that Wittgenstein's primary concern is with meaning, explanations of meaning and use. This is fully evident in the subsequent application he makes of these general reflections on rule-following in the private language argument.

Wittgenstein's discussion of rules and their applications is skilfully crafted to accomplish his limited strategic purpose. This can be made clear by narrowing *our* focus to the special case of the internal relations between explanations of word-meaning and uses of words. Four points then stand out. First, the observation that rules are canons of correctness for actions boils down to the claim that explanations of meaning are the standards we employ in classifying uses of words as correct or incorrect. This, of course, is a fundamental justification for bringing explanations of meaning under the label 'rules'. Secondly, the fact that applying a rule correctly is a criterion for understanding it and that misapplying it is a criterion for misunderstanding it (cf. §201) is reflected down on to the principle that how one uses a word is a criterion for how an explanation of meaning is understood. In earlier criticism of the Augustinian picture, Wittgenstein had already stressed this point. Whether an ostensive definition is understood or mis-understood is manifested in how the defined word is used (§§28f., cf. §§122ff.). Thirdly and consequently, understand-ing an explanation (understanding a rule) is just knowing how to use the explained word correctly (knowing how to apply the rule). The illusion that the concept of meaning is split in two by the twin relations to explanation and use is shattered by noting that giving an explanation which one understands and using a word correctly in the knowledge that the uses made of it are correct are not two separate things, but two aspects of a single capacity. Correct uses of a word are criteria both for understanding an explanation of it and for knowing how to use it correctly. Fourthly, the internal connection between knowing how to use a word and the ability to explain what it means is a special case of the internal relation between following a rule and being able to state the rule that one is following. The idea that understanding words transcends speakers' abilities to explain their meanings (§§75ff.) should appear just as problematic as the idea that agents may act with the intention of following rules without being able to say what rules they are following. The argument against constructing theories in philosophy is absorbed into the general contention that there are no *hidden* rules, that rules do not act at a distance.

4   The harmony between language and reality

Recognizing the nature of the internal relations between a rule and its applications, and its implications for a correct conception of the relations of meaning, use and explanation, undercuts two perennial temptations to philosophical error. One is to erect a mythology of symbolism or symbolic processes. This is exemplified here in the thought that rules, in some mysterious way, contain their own applications (as Platonists are inclined to think that the axioms of geometry 'contain' within themselves all the theorems). The rule of an arithmetical series seems then to determine what consequences flow from it; all we humans do is draw forth from the rule what is already there independently of us. The other great temptation is to construct a mythology of mental or psychological processes; for example, to suppose that the expression of a rule is endowed with a role in distinguishing correct from incorrect actions only in virtue of mental acts of meaning which we perform.

Correctly characterizing the relation of a rule to its applications as internal is to deny that it makes sense to speak of any essential intermediate entities between a rule and its applications. Neither acts of meaning nor interpretations cement a rule to its consequences. But nor is a rule a queer logical machine which contains its applications in advance of being applied. Internal relations are not explained by recourse to the mysteries of the mind, nor are they explained by invoking super-physical mechanisms of a Platonist kind. Internal relations are the product of grammar, of linguistic conventions. Clarifying these is bedrock in philosophical elucidation of concepts. Trying to dig deeper leads to metaphysical and psychological mythology.

Viewed thus, Wittgenstein's remarks on rule-following take on a wider significance. The relation between rules and actions is merely one aspect of a larger problem that dominated his reflections, the problems of 'the harmony between language and reality'. Indeed, the characterization of explanations of meaning as rules for using expressions and the connection made between explanation and the concept of meaning ensure that any account of the general harmony between language and reality would plainly be incomplete unless it explicitly covered the harmony between rules and actions. Conversely, discussions elsewhere of other aspects of this general harmony may contribute material important to the understanding of this part of the *Philosophical Investigations*; for there is a host of parallels among other chains of reasoning and in the philosophical consequences derived from them. As well as points of detail, the smooth subsumption of the remarks on rule-following into the framework of Wittgenstein's discussions of the harmony between language and reality puts a final nail in the coffin of the rule-sceptical interpretation of these observations. Everything testifies against his construing the clarification of the relations of propositions to facts, of orders to their executions, of desires or expectations and their fulfilments, etc., as being concerned with upholding or refuting scepticism in any form. On the contrary, everything speaks for the claim that his concerns in these remarks were purely logical. The harmony between language and the world is, as it were, antecedent to questions of doubt and certainty.

Wittgenstein's original fascination with this harmony is evident in the picture theory of meaning in the *Tractatus*. He attributed to the world a logical structure isomorphic with the structure of language (when fully analysed). A proposition connects with the world by presenting a logical picture of a state of affairs, and its truth consists in the realization of this possible state of affairs, i.e. in its being a fact. The possibility of meaningful discourse was grounded in a metaphysical correspondence between language and reality. For this reason, many of his later reflections on this putative harmony took the form of reconsidering the claim that a proposition is (or contains) a picture of the fact which verifies it if it is true (and such parallel claims as that a command contains a picture of its execution). He frequently reworked a distinctive line of criticism. He had rightly perceived that the relation between a proposition and the fact that makes it true is internal. But he had been mistaken in thinking it to be something metaphysical and a victim of mystification in thinking it to be ineffable. When he wrote the *Tractatus* he had thought that such statements as 'A proposition is true if it corresponds to the facts' or 'The proposition that p is true if and only if it is a fact that p' expressed (or were attempts to express) metaphysical truths about the relationship between language and the world. Now he realized that like all apparently metaphysical harmonies, this 'harmony' is forged in grammar. The statement that a proposition is true if it corresponds to the facts is not a metaphysical truth about the relations of language and reality; nor is it false (as those who correctly repudiate the Correspondence Theory of Truth suppose). It is rather a grammatical truism, a reflection of the grammatical rule that for most purposes one can replace the phrase 'a true proposition' by the phrase 'a proposition that corresponds to the facts'. Similarly 'the proposition that p is true if and only if it is a fact that p' plumbs no metaphysical profundities. It merely reflects the grammatical rule that instead of the phrase 'the fact that p' we can use the phrase 'the fact that makes the proposition that p true'. So the 'harmony between language and reality' is no more than a reflection, a shadow of a rule for the use of signs, a grammatical convention.[15]

Just as the impressive harmony between language and reality dissolves into an unimpressive truism, so too the pressure to introduce third entities to mediate between the relata of an internal relation is similarly relieved by more careful scrutiny of grammatical articulations. We realize dimly that there is an internal relation between a proposition that we propound (a sentence-in-use) and the fact that makes it true. But that fact may not obtain. Yet even then, we are inclined to think, the proposition still describes *something* (it does not describe nothing!) Moreover it must surely describe the very thing we believe when we believe it to be true. For, if the fact that p, unbeknownst to us, does not obtain, we may still believe that p. So what we believe cannot be a fact, but only something very close to a fact, e.g. a possible state of affairs. And of this 'possible state of affairs' philosophers make a shadowy intermediary between sentence-in-use and a fact, viz. the *sense* of a sentence (or 'proposition' in a Platonist sense). This too is an illusion, which we foist on ourselves as a result of misconstruing the grammar of our language.[16] For we take the 'object' of belief or thought to be akin to the object of expectation in the sentence 'I expect John'; and this in turn seems akin to the object of shooting as in 'I shot John', but yet mysteriously different. For while I cannot shoot John if he is not there, I can expect him even though he is not there. We fail to see the relationship between 'I expect John' and 'I expect that John will come', and we are inclined to treat the phrase 'that he will come' as the name of an 'object' of belief, thought or expectation just as 'John' is the name of an object; only the object of belief is a little more aethereal.

A further important source of the philosophical tendency to interpose intermediate entities in order to explain internal

---

[15] Cf. Wittgenstein, *Philosophical Grammar*, ed. Rush Rhees (Blackwell, Oxford, 1974), pp. 161f.

[16] Cf. Wittgenstein, *The Blue and Brown Books* (Blackwell, Oxford, 1969), pp. 31ff.

relations lies in yet deeper misconceptions about the nature and limits of representation. In the *Tractatus* this was embodied in the doctrines of analysis and isomorphism, viz. the representing proposition, *when fully analysed*, must contain just as many elements as are present in what is represented. The rules of logical syntax and the correlation of the simple names with simple objects in reality ensured that the proposition is a logical picture of what it represents. Isomorphism and identical logical multiplicity were thought to be the key to the possibility of representation. This too, Wittgenstein later realized, was an illusion. It is the ordinary proposition (sentence-in-use) that represents, not some hidden hitherto unknown refinement of it. And the thesis of isomorphism stemmed (in part) from an absurd attempt *to write into the picture (the representing symbol) the method (or technique) of its projection*. The consequence of this criticism is to reduce the bold claim that any representation must have something in common with what it represents (viz. logical multiplicity and logical form) to the vacuity that what is projected must be projectible.[17] And, of course, the familiar sentence is just as projectible as its mythical depth-analysans.

A multitude of further arguments are to be found scattered through the pages of Wittgenstein's later writings, all fragments of an attack, sometimes direct, sometimes indirect, on mythologies of symbolism attractive to philosophers.[18] These arguments do not call into question the legitimacy of speaking of propositions or the senses of sentences, or of insisting that true propositions are those which correspond to the facts. Rather, they show that these expressions cannot be construed as designating entities which have any intelligible role in resolving philosophical perplexity. On the contrary, thus construed they re-introduce the very perplexities they were meant to remove, adding a dollop of mystification for good

[17] Wittgenstein, *Philosophical Grammar*, p. 163.
[18] Some of these had certainly attracted Wittgenstein when he was composing the *Tractatus*, but it would be quite mistaken to think that all the illusions and confusions he discusses were the intellectual sins of his youth.

measure. Introduced in the course of an attempt to *explain* internal relations, they accomplish less than nothing.

This battery of arguments dissolving the mysteries of the Great Harmony between Language and the World is not repeated in the remarks on rules in the *Investigations*, but many of those remarks run parallel to, or echo, earlier arguments on the broader front. The strange illusion that a rule must, in some sense, foreshadow any act that is in conformity with it runs parallel to the idea that a sentence-in-use, a proposition, must, in some way, foreshadow the fact that will make it true. The supposition that internal relations must be cemented by means of an intermediate entity (e.g. a state of affairs, the sense of a sentence, the object of belief) is paralleled by the idea that an interpretation must mediate between a rule and its application. And the metaphysical mystification involved in postulating a state of affairs as the sense of a sentence, which is so close to a fact that it is a shadow of the fact (virtually identical with it save for a Yes or No!) is paralleled in the case of rules. For once one realizes that any interpretation hangs in the air along with what it interprets, one is tempted to locate the *ultimate interpretation* in the mind (the last refuge of the philosophical scoundrel). Meaning thus-and-so, we are inclined to think, really can *uniquely* anticipate reality, can contain the applications of a rule in advance. Meaning, as Wittgenstein put it in the *Blue Book* (p. 34) 'is the last interpretation'. The criticism of the picture theory of meaning (the requirement of isomorphism and identical logical multiplicity) that it absurdly attempted to incorporate the technique of projection into the picture has a faint echo in criticism of the idea that a rule must in some sense contain its applications, that the *real* rule of the series of even integers must contain, e.g. '1000, 1002, 1004 . . .', perhaps, in some sense, encapsulated in the general formula of the rule, in some Platonic realm, or in the mind. Here too the fallacy turns on failure to apprehend *the use of the rule as a standard of correctness*, the technique of applying the rule. We fail to see that to understand the rule-formulation is not to grasp something that mysteriously contains a picture of its own applications, but rather to grasp a technique of application (hence something dynamic, not static!). In these and other ways, the *Investigations* reverberates with the echoes of previous philosophical campaigns, applying, modifying, and improving on earlier tactical successes.

A second form of harmony is intimately related to the harmony between language and reality, namely the harmony between *thought* and reality. Again, the origins of Wittgenstein's fascination with this issue lie in the picture theory of meaning. Two quite different roles were assigned to the mind in the *Tractatus*. One was to effect the connection between names and objects, i.e. to bestow meanings on the indefinables of language. Language is projected on to the world in thought. But this 'thinking out of the method of projection' cannot be expressed in propositions; it was held to be ineffable. The second role of the mind was manifest in Wittgenstein's attempt to explain the intentionality of propositional attitudes, e.g. believing, wishing, hoping, and expecting that such–and–such is the case. It seemed that the essential component of any propositional attitude is the picture of its object. For how else can I know what it is that I expect later to happen, how can I believe what is not the case or wish for what has not yet come to pass. Wittgenstein tried to *explain* the manifest internal relation between propositional attitudes and what satisfies them (the fact that makes the belief that p true, the event that satisfies the expectation that p, etc.) by a picture theory of the mind. He apparently held that to think (expect, believe, wish) that p is to be in a certain psychological state. This state, he held, must incorporate the thought that p (even if it is not a fact that p, I still think that p). This seemed possible only if the psychological state consisted *inter alia* of psychical constituents in a structure that is isomorphic with (the analysed form of) the proposition 'p'. For only then would it contain a picture of what will satisfy it. It is possible therefore to think, believe, hope or expect what is not the case, or what is yet to come, precisely because the thought, belief, hope or expectation consists of psychic elements that picture a possible state of affairs, namely just that state of affairs that is realized in the fact that would make the thought or belief true, the hope or expectation fulfilled. In short, A's thought that *p* is itself treated as an expression, but as one in mental symbols rather than perceptible ones.[19] The harmony between thought and reality is forged by means of psychic structures (logical pictures in the language of thought).[20]

Here too Wittgenstein's later reflections on this apparently metaphysical harmony took the form of reconsidering the pictoriality of the putative mental states of thinking, expecting, desiring, willing, intending, etc. This work embraces much of his extensive writings on philosophy of mind. Here we can only sketch in the most general contours of his thinking. He criticized the earlier idea that what is meant (the projecting of language on to reality) is ineffable. The mind has no magical powers to link names to objects. Whatever may be meant in a putative act of meaning (*Meinen*) can be expressed (and must be expressible) in an explanation of meaning. And such acts of meaning can accomplish nothing which an explanation cannot in principle also accomplish.

The earlier idea that a thought consists of psychic constituents which symbolize a possible state of affairs involves many confusions. Of course, the underlying insight that there is an internal relation between thought and reality was correct. But the supposition that this must be explained by psychic isomorphism and multiplicity was a product of confusion, an attempt to explain a grammatical connection by conjuring up a mythical, non-linguistic, entity to mediate between believing, thinking, expecting, etc. and what makes the thought or belief

---

[19] Cf. Wittgenstein, *Tractatus*, 3.1–3.12, 5.541–5.542 and *Notebooks 1914–1916* (Blackwell, Oxford, 1961), Appendix III, p. 129; see also A. J. P. Kenny, 'Wittgenstein's Early Philosophy of Mind' in *Perspectives on the Philosophy of Wittgenstein* ed. I. Block (Blackwell, Oxford, 1981).

[20] Cognitive psychology is only now catching up with these (fallacious) doctrines. It will, doubtless, take many more decades for it to discover that its apparently up to date patter about 'mental representations' and 'the language of thought' is a poor variant of a long-since exploded fallacy.

true, or fulfils the expectation. The array of psychic constituents (arranged according to rules of logical syntax!) and isomorphic with the state of affairs represented is a fiction. For
expectation and the event expected, hope and its fulfilment, or
belief and what renders it true make contact in grammar, not
via a shadowy psychic intermediary. The unmediated internal
relation between a propositional attitude and what satisfies it is
a reflection of a grammatical relation between the *expression* of
the propositional attitude and the *description* of its satisfaction.
Thinking, believing, intending, willing, etc. are not typically
mental states at all, and it makes no sense to conceive of them
as complexes composed of psychic constituents. Somebody
who says 'I'm going to London tomorrow' expresses his
intention, but does not describe anything, *a fortiori* not a state
of mind. The intention expressed is: A's intention to go to
London tomorrow. And that intention *is* (is identical with) the
intention that is satisfied by A's going to London tomorrow.
A's now expecting E to happen does not need any intermediary
to cement its internal relation to E. For it is a rule of grammar
that 'A's expecting E to happen' = 'The expectation of A that
is satisfied by E's happening'. The harmony between thought
and reality is orchestrated in grammar.[21]

The echoes of these extensive reflections about the mind are,
as would be expected, muted in *Investigations* §§185–242. It is
rules, their formulations and applications that occupy centre
stage. But some of the illusions generated by philosophical
reflections on normativity run parallel to those dissolved
earlier. The idea that an act of meaning mediates between a
rule and its application is in effect criticized by the argument
that an intention does not in some magical way foreshadow an
act that executes it (§186ff.). The *reductio ad absurdum* of the
suggestion that an interpretation must mediate between rule

---

[21] Note, in passing, that this multifaceted issue has nothing to do with
scepticism. What makes a thought true, executes an intention, fulfils a
desire, etc. is no more problematic or uncertain than what description of a
state of affairs meshes with the expression of a thought, intention or desire.
And this is absolutely perspicuous.

and application is parallel to earlier criticisms of fictitious intermediate entities cementing internal relations. A correct conception of the harmony between thought and reality removes all the allure from the prospect of trying to understand the nature of the relations between rules and applications by means of a digression through mental states or acts.

5 *Übersicht*

The outcome of these reflections on the grand strategy of the *Investigations* is of great general significance. First, the remarks on rule-following are located within a ramifying network of earlier argument (some of which reappears later in the *Investigations* too) on the topic of philosophical misconceptions about the harmony between language and reality. They have every appearance of constituting a division within an army engaged on a large-scale campaign. Secondly, they are by no means a straightforward rehashing of arguments marshalled elsewhere in discussions of internal relations. New arguments are deployed here in pursuit of different quarries. The discussion of the internal relations between rules and their applications here is an essential phase in coordinating the concepts of explanation of meaning (rules for the use of expressions) and of use. (In the *Remarks on the Foundations of Mathematics* the same manoeuvres, more comprehensively executed and differently ordered, are put to yet another purpose.) Appreciation of these two points should remove any temptation to interpret Wittgenstein's discussion as being an elaboration of a new form of scepticism and a countervailing sceptical solution.

Resistance to the idea that the internal relations between language and reality are mere shadows of grammar, or that the seemingly adamantine links which appear to be what makes representation possible are no more than reflections of linguistic conventions, rules for the use of signs, is powerful and deeply engrained in philosophers. We quite naturally adhere to a captivating picture that words, sentences and symbols constitute a separate realm of entities (parallel to the realm of mental phenomena) which stands over and against the realm of objects, events, facts, states of affairs, actions, etc. It seems as if language and the world are divided each from the other by a metaphysical gulf. And it seems that if it is possible (as it surely is) to *represent reality* in thought and language at all, then this gulf must be bridged. The suggestion that the harmony between language and reality is no more than a matter of grammatical convention seems ludicrous, a misguided trivialization of what is deepest and most important in philosophy. The world is one thing, language is another. If the bridge between them, the connection of language and reality, is merely the shadow of grammatical rules, then there is no bridge between them. For the shadow of a bridge is not a bridge. The pits of Idealism, Solipsism, Scepticism suddenly yawn open at our very feet!

The captivating picture which we so unreflectively accept and unthinkingly cleave to is the most general target of Wittgenstein's later philosophy. It is the ultimate foundation of the Augustinian picture of language. And, strikingly, it is the moving spirit behind the modern conviction that statements in a metalanguage are the only conceivable means for constructing a rigorous scientific theory of meaning for a language. Wittgenstein struggles to free us from its hold over us. A language is an aspect of human *action*, rooted in human *behaviour*. It did not emerge from some kind of ratiocination.[22] Speaking is acting; and uttering words and sentences is interwoven with human activities taking place within the world of which we are a part. A language in use is part of a form of life. These are platitudes; no one in his right mind would deny them. The difficulty is not in recognizing their truth, but in viewing them from the right perspective, seeing the philosophical implications of these truisms, and apprehending how the houses of cards we are so deeply inclined to build in our

[22] Wittgenstein, *On Certainty* (Blackwell, Oxford, 1969), §475.

attempts to answer philosophical questions are premised on their tacit or explicit denial.

Symbols are not to be set over against the world, as if sounds and signs were not elements in the world. Of course, we dimly realize that 'mere' sounds and signs are not symbols. They must be infused with life; and this life-endowing role we attribute to the mind (which, we are inclined to think, is also set over against the world). But what gives signs their life, what makes them symbols, is the role we give them, the use we make of them, in our daily linguistic transactions. We *use* (parts of) the world to represent the world. This is, perhaps, most evident in the case of 'concrete' symbols. Samples, paradigms (such as colour samples, standard weights and measures) are parts of our *means of representation*. They play an essential role in explanations of meaning and hence are commonly employed in expressions of standards of correctness for the use of words. When we use a ruler to measure the length of a table, or a book of colour samples to identify a particular kind of paint we need, do we feel that there is a gulf between language and reality? And when we use a sample as part of our *means of communication* (as in 'I saw some material of this ↑ pattern' or 'Bring me some paint of this ↑ colour') do we feel that we have crossed a metaphysical bridge in thought?

Nothing is a symbol at all in isolation from practices that endow it with *potentialities of use* in human affairs. (And nothing is a rule-formulation in abstraction from its recognized use as an expression of a standard of correctness in conduct.) Abstracting a language from this background of activities and events removes all justification for speaking of *symbols* at all. There is no such thing as a language in isolation from these worldly transactions. The metaphysical gulf between language and reality is a philosophical illusion.

How then is language connected to reality? The question continues stubbornly to bewilder us. And when Wittgenstein answers bluntly: 'There is *no* connection between language and reality', we react with astonishment. If there is no such connection, then how can we represent the world? And we thus construe Wittgenstein's ideas within the framework of thought that he was trying to demolish. For, we think, if the harmony between language and reality is merely the shadow of grammar, then there is not really *any* harmony between language and reality. And now, it seems, we are locked within the kaleidoscope of language. And we take Wittgenstein to subscribe to a form of linguistic idealism, a sort of 'communal solipsism'.[23] For from this distorted perspective, grammar seems to be able to fulfil the role of *apparently* bridging the gulf between language and reality only if reality, as it appears to us, is itself the creation or product of the rules of grammar. On this view language is not a method of representation of something external and independent, but rather the world we apprehend is a product of our means of representation (just as Kant's phenomenal world was conceived as the product of the interaction of unknowable things–in–themselves with the structures imposed by the mind). In so far as grammar is shared among the speakers of a single language, reality will be a public and community–wide creation of grammar. But in so far as grammar is a collection of decisions or stipulations, reality will depend upon us.

The ground is cut out from under these deep philosophical misunderstandings (and gross misinterpretations of Wittgenstein) once it is recognized that they are not viable in the light of Wittgenstein's repudiation of the conception of language and reality as two discrete, self–contained realms of being. If the gulf between language and reality is illusory, then of course no bridge can span it. The statement that there is no connection between language and reality is not the affirmation of an antithesis to the thesis that they are connected by some mysterious mental or metaphysical bridging apparatus. It is rather a denial that there is room for any connection, for there is no gulf to span. The question 'How is language connected to

[23] Cf. B. Williams, 'Wittgenstein and Idealism' in *Understanding Wittgenstein*, Royal Institute of Philosophy Lectures, vol. 7, 1972–3, ed. G. Vesey (Macmillan, London, 1974).

reality?' is what is amiss. For it rests firmly on a misconceived picture. Wittgenstein's account does not throw open a back door to further metaphysical speculations, but shows there is no exit from the business of clarifying the grammar of our concepts. A philosopher who persists in thinking the relation of an understood rule to its indefinite, unlimited range of applications to be a deep mystery calling for the production of ingenious and sophisticated philosophical theories – such a philosopher has not entered into the rich legacy of Wittgenstein's philosophical investigations.

Index

List of the main discussions of sections from
Philosophical Investigations, Part I: